# The Return: As In Moses' Day, It Will Be At Jesus Christ's Coming

# The Return: As In Moses' Day, It Will Be At Jesus Christ's Coming

*ARLIN EWALD NUSBAUM*

ALPHA AND OMEGA PUBLISHING

Copyright 2024

Alpha & Omega Publishing

All rights reserved.

Ebook ISBN: 978-1-60135-872-1
Print BW ISBN: 978-1-60135-873-8

https://lionandlamb.net

## Contents

| | |
|---|---|
| Preface | 7 |
| Introduction | 9 |
| Shadows & Types | 17 |
| Bondage | 19 |
| Feasts | 36 |
| Darkness | 54 |
| Waters Divided | 58 |
| Split Rock | 60 |
| Fiery Serpent | 62 |
| Eagles' Wings | 67 |
| Lands of Promise | 71 |
| Signs & Wonders | 102 |
| A Prophet | 129 |
| God | 133 |
| Glory | 171 |
| Deception | 182 |
| Wealth Transfer | 185 |
| Conclusion | 191 |
| Appendix: Shekinah References | 196 |

# PREFACE

This updated edition of *The Return* is now part of the *Testimony Series*.

https://Testimony.Vision

Back in 2014, God gave me an assignment by His audible voice. It came from within and without. It was as if God turned my body into a megaphone, shaking every cell in my body. This is what His voice said,

> The Return: As it was in the days of Moses, so shall it be at the Coming of the Son of Man. Learn what that means, and write about it.

I received other forms of Divine Assistance while researching *The Return*, which were not mentioned in the first edition. When reading the part where Moses split the rock in Horeb and water came forth, I was allowed to witness that for a *future* purpose, which was not disclosed for *5 years* with the writing of *Temple Mount 11:11 Horn of God*.

# INTRODUCTION

It has been a decade since the first edition was published in 2014. At that time, Christians still had a great interest in the Antichrist. But before that, I'd had a profound experience with Our Lord that shifted my focus off the enemy.

I shall never forget that day, it was July 4$^{th}$ 2002. I was camping alone and had just completed a book assignment. Quite unexpectedly, Our Lord took me out of my body high above Earth, and while both of us were there hovering, He pointed at the Earth and said,

> Look at the number of My Followers.

They were represented as bright dots of light and seemed to number in the billions. Then, a percentage of those lights dimmed, and Our Lord said,

> Look how many of them are waiting for the coming of the Antichrist.

Then the lights dimmed even more, and He said,

> Those are My Followers who are looking for My return.

I noted they were few compared with the other two groups. Then I took note of His displeasure with the situation, and He said,

I am calling you to change the focus of My Followers from an anticpation of the Antichrist to My coming glory.

He then returned me to Earth, and I was left to ponder my new assignment and what I was shown. Later, I learned that a significant part of that problem stems from prophecy writers (books and films). Readers may recall the *Left Behind* series of books and movies; there is even a series for teenagers.

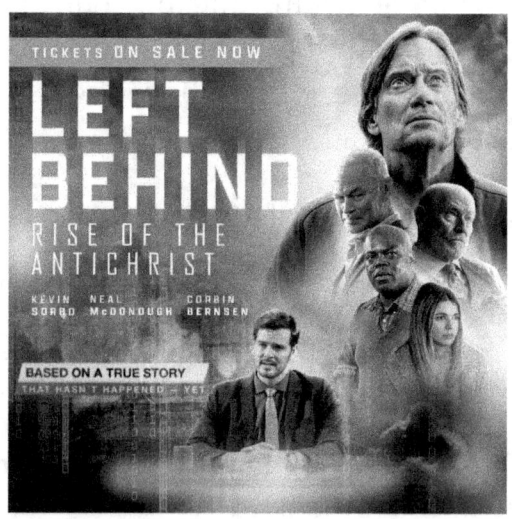

*Left Behind Movie Poster*

They hyped the Antichrist and, by doing so, had spread an incorrect prophetic model. The closest prophetic model presented in films that focus on Our Lord is Rapture-centric.

When Our Lord said to focus on His "coming glory," The word *glory* stood out to me. That redirected my attention from His coming in general to the coming of His glory in specifics, and I sought to learn all that I could of that glory's different forms and manifestations.

For example, did you know the prophecy about the "Sign of His coming" is about His coming *glory*?

> 30 And then shall appear the **SIGN of the Son of man in heaven**: and then shall all the tribes of the earth mourn, and they shall see the Son of man coming in the clouds of heaven **with power and GREAT GLORY.** (Matthew 24)

I learned there was a *potential* prophetic outcome for Earth that could entirely bypass the horrors in the Revelation of John.

> 28 For he will finish the work, and **CUT it SHORT in RIGHTEOUSNESS:** because a short work will the Lord make upon the earth. (Romans 9)

Our Lord gave me additional insights about this perspective, which I included in my book *Cut Short in Righteousness* (2014). After writing *The Return* in 2014, I wrote the following books.

- *Quickened Within, Mystery of the Inner Man* (2015)
- *Babylon – Then and Now* (2016)
- *The Joy-Filled Way* (2016)
- *The World With God* (2016)
- *Millennial Dawn* (2017)

- *Prophecy Wars: The Prophecy War Will End All Wars & Stop the Antichrist* (2017)
- *The Age of Illumination – Compendium* (2017)
- *Bread of Life* (2017)
- *A Higher Form of Existence* (2017)
- *The Remnant* (2017)
- *D5 – His GLORY Shall APPEAR to Your JOY, to Their SHAME* (2018)

The task of shifting people's focus off the Antichrist onto the coming *Glory* of Our Lord was a success. His coming Glory replaced the Antichrist as the centerpiece of prophetic expectation. Many modern prophets, if not all, were prophesying about the coming Glory, not doom, gloom, or the Antichrist.

However, no one wrote more on the topic than myself (books and websites), and our young family grew up with that prophetic expectation. Then everything came to a halt by a miserable series of events that began with the COVID lockdowns and ended with the stealing of the 2020 Election.[1]

In short, that prophetic outcome was tied to the United States staying on course with President Trump, but sadly, that did not happen. I began to ask Our Lord to intercede by the prophesied removal of the (absolute) wicked. I justified my requests with the many prophecies and our current needs[2] to save America.

Our Lord affirmed those prophecies were accurate and even went so far as to inform me of the day they would be fulfilled on *Thanksgiving Day* (2020). Only those who lived through the uncertainties of the 2020 Election know how spiritually dark it was. Every attempt to correct voting errors was thwarted. Hope was lost, and evil won. The evil was so thick it was tangible to anyone with discernment.

Thanksgiving came and left, America was not saved, the (absolute) wicked were not destroyed, and I wanted some answers. But Our Lord was not quick to respond, which made it worse. When He finally spoke, He asked that I go to a local McDonalds where He said, "All would be revealed." So I drove to that McDonalds, and there wasn't a single customer inside.

I went in, sat in the center of the dining area, and waited. Then, all at once, *five* dads with their young sons and daughters came in, yet none knew the other. After ordering their food, they sat on all sides of me. There was no background music; it was a very somber scene. With that, Our Lord had my full attention.

Then He explained why He did not "pull the trigger." He said what I observed would have been multiplied by the millions: husbands without wives and children without mothers, and a new set of God-haters would have emerged.

At that moment, I experienced a *paradigm shift* that was not composed of just one new concept but several. Our Lord chose to sacrifice the physical comforts of the Saved to give the Lost more time. This is echoed in the following parable that Our Lord gave during His ministry.

> 4 What man of you, having an hundred sheep, if he lose one of them, doth not **leave the ninety and nine** in the wilderness, and **go after that which is LOST,** until he find it? (Luke 15)

So, the faithful (and the public) have had to endure one continuous nightmare after another under the Biden Presidency, and the world will not be saved from the horrors of the Revelation of John by a *Cut Short in Righteousness* outcome. However, the Return of Our Lord's Glory IS still on track, with some modifications. Part of that dynamic is this:

> 6 Give not that which is holy unto the dogs, **neither cast ye your PEARLS BEFORE SWINE**, lest they trample them under their feet, and turn again and rend you. (Matthew 7)

> 32 And when they **heard of the resurrection of the dead, SOME MOCKED.** (Acts 17)

> 18 How that they told you **there should be MOCKERS in the LAST TIME** (Jude 1)

I began researching all things about Moses and the children of Israel. I learned that their story is unique, but not in the ways traditionally held with Moses delivering the children of Israel out of Egypt, the parting of the Red Sea, and the destruction of Pharaoh and his army. Without question, those *were* remarkable events, but they were not as extraordinary as others I would discover. The children of Israel would be delivered from bondage on many occasions, and the Jordan River was parted three times (Jos 3:16, 2Kgs 2:8,14).

What I found peculiar about Moses and the children of Israel was God's appearing to them on Mt. Sinai. So far as I could tell, this was the most unique part. The details Moses gave were very particular; it's as if he knew that one day, they would be necessary for a future generation to understand. UFO enthusiasts seem to be most interested in that part of their story. They believe it is proof that UFOs exist and God uses them. However, this interpretation may prove too simplistic as it would rob God of His glory and power, preventing readers from knowing Him for who He truly is.

There are many contemporary accounts, whether they are near-death experiences (NDE), dreams, visions, or out-of-body visits to Heaven, where people observed God upon His throne, and what they relate is very similar to what Moses described happening at Mt. Sinai. If individuals in Heaven are seeing what Moses and the children of Israel saw, but *without* a UFO present, then Moses and the children of Israel probably did see God. I learned this is an important distinction to understand as it pertains to "the return" and who and what will return.

People today are in just as much bondage as the

children of Israel were, but we have not realized this, nor has anyone made the correlation until now. God sent "fiery serpents" among the children of Israel to mend them of their ingratitude. That part of their story is analogous to the prophesied Antichrist and Beast System. And just as God gave the wealth of the Egyptians to the children of Israel, so too is that comparable to the faithful "inheriting the Earth" and its wealth.

What is essential to know is that the whole chronicle of Moses and the children of Israel is a *Type, shadow,* or *blueprint* that was *foreordained* by God to show us what will happen in our day and to help us prepare for it. There isn't a more extraordinary event than what is about to hit the Earth.

Notes

1. See my book EXODUS (2022).
2. See my books *Tabera* (2017) and *Taken* (2022) for details.

# SHADOWS & TYPES

The belief that God uses examples from the past to foreshadow things of the future is called *Typology*.

> **Typology**: the doctrine or study of *Types* or prefigurative symbols, especially in scriptural literature. –*Random House Dictionary*

According to the title of this book, which was given by the voice of God: *The Return: As In Moses' Day, It Will Be At Jesus Christ's Coming*; I take this as proof that God does use *Types*. Here are some verses that support their use.

> 14 Nevertheless death reigned from Adam to Moses, even over them that had not sinned after the similitude of Adam's transgression, who is the **figure** of him that was to come. (Romans 5)

> 5 For if we have been planted together in the **likeness** of his death, we shall be also in the **likeness** of his resurrection: (Romans 6)

> 6 Now these things were our **examples**, to the intent we should not lust after evil things, as they also lusted. (1 Corinthians 10)

> 17 Which are a **shadow** of things to come; (Colossians 2)

15 And it is yet far more evident: for that after the **similitude** of Melchisedec there ariseth another priest, (Hebrews 7)

5 Who serve unto the **example** and **shadow** of heavenly things, as Moses was admonished of God when he was about to make the tabernacle: for, See, saith he, that thou make all things according to the pattern shewed to thee in the mount. (Hebrews 8)

9 Which was a **figure** for the time then present, in which were offered both gifts and sacrifices, that could not make him that did the service perfect, as pertaining to the conscience; (Hebrews 9)

1 For the law having a **shadow** of good things to come, and not the very image of the things, can never with those sacrifices which they offered year by year continually make the comers thereunto perfect. (Hebrews 10)

I started identifying as many *Types* as possible from the account of Moses and the children of Israel, and I found that they make up a significant portion of this book. The first one I learned about was "bondage," reviewed next.

# BONDAGE

An essential part of the story of Moses and the children of Israel was their deliverance from *bondage* under the yoke of the Egyptians. However, the type of enslavement most people associate with the Israelites is *physical*. I discovered other types of bondage and the apostle Paul identified them.

In the following stanza, Paul confirms the title's premise that God uses *Types* and encourages us not to be ignorant of the account of the children of Israel. Notably, Paul said they are for "us" upon whom the "ends of the world have come."

> 1 Moreover, brethren, **I would not that ye should be ignorant**, how that all our fathers were under the cloud, and all passed through the sea;
> 5 But with **many of them God was not well pleased**: for they were overthrown in the wilderness.
> 6 Now **these things were our examples**, to the intent we should **not lust after evil things**, as they also lusted.
> 7 **Neither be ye idolaters**, as were some of them; as it is written, The people sat down to eat and drink, and rose up to play.
> 8 **Neither let us commit fornication**, as some of them committed, and fell in one day three and twenty thousand.

9 **Neither let us tempt Christ**, as some of them also tempted, and were destroyed of serpents.

10 **Neither murmur ye**, as some of them also murmured, and were destroyed of the destroyer.

11 **Now all these things happened unto them for ensamples**: and they are **written for our admonition, upon whom the ends of the world are come.** (1 Corinthians 10)

Not wanting to be ignorant, I did as Paul suggested and extracted the different kinds of bondage, particularly those not commonly associated with Moses and the children of Israel.

## DON'T CRAVE CARNAL THINGS

6 Now these things were our examples, to the intent we **should not lust after evil things**, as they also lusted. (1 Corinthians 10:6)

6 Now these things occurred as examples to keep us from **setting our hearts on evil things** as they did. (NIV)

6 These things happened as a warning to us, so that we would **not crave evil things** as they did, (NLT)

6 Now these things are examples (warnings and admonitions) for us **not to desire or crave or covet or lust after evil and carnal things** as they did. (AMP)

## Background

The background to this warning is that the children of Israel craved *flesh* instead of the *manna* God provided. In turn, God gave them so much flesh it was "yet between their teeth" when they died of the plague.

> 4 And the mixed multitude that was among them **fell a lusting**: and the children of Israel also **wept again**, and said, **Who shall give us flesh to eat?**
> 13 Whence should I have flesh to give unto all this people? for **they weep unto me**, saying, **Give us flesh, that we may eat.**
> 18 And say thou unto the people, Sanctify yourselves against to morrow, and ye shall eat flesh: for **ye have wept in the ears of the Lord**, saying, Who shall give us flesh to eat? for it was well with us in Egypt: therefore the Lord will give you flesh, and ye shall eat.
> 19 Ye shall not eat one day, nor two days, nor five days, neither ten days, nor twenty days;
> 20 But even a **whole month, until it come out at your nostrils**, and it be loathsome unto you: because that **ye have despised the Lord which is among you**, and have wept before him, saying, Why came we forth out of Egypt?
> 31 And there went forth a wind from the Lord, and brought quails from the sea, and let them fall by the camp, as it were a day's journey on this side, and as it were a day's journey on the other side, round about the camp, and as

it were **two cubits high upon the face of the Earth.**

32 And the people stood up all that day, and all that night, and all the next day, and they gathered the quails: he that gathered least gathered ten homers: and they spread them all abroad for themselves round about the camp.

33 And **while the flesh was yet between their teeth, ere it was chewed, the wrath of the Lord was kindled against the people, and the Lord smote the people with a very great plague.**

34 And he called the name of that place Kibroth-hattaavah: because **there they buried the people that lusted.** (Numbers 11)

The lust of the flesh can be a canker to the soul. We are not here to become slaves, addicted to our cravings, having no remorse for the needless slaughter of God's animals. Even in God's presence, they "served the creature more than the Creator" (Rom. 1:25).

We, who will be here to transition into The Millennium, should be mindful that there was no eating of flesh in the Garden of Eden or Heaven, and there will be none in The Millennium.

> 6 The wolf also shall dwell with the lamb, and the leopard shall lie down with the kid; and the calf and the young lion and the fatling together; and a little child shall lead them.
>
> 7 And the cow and the bear shall feed; their young ones shall lie down together: and the

**lion shall eat straw like the ox.**
8 And the sucking child shall play on the hole of the asp, and the weaned child shall put his hand on the cockatrice' den.
9 **They shall not hurt nor destroy in all my holy mountain:** for the earth shall be full of the knowledge of the Lord, as the waters cover the sea. (Isaiah 11)

## DON'T BE IDOLATERS

7 **Neither be ye idolaters**, as were some of them; (1 Corinthians 10)

7 **Do not be worshipers of false gods** as some of them were, as it is written, The people sat down to eat and drink [the sacrifices offered to the golden calf at Horeb] and rose to sport (to dance and give way to jesting and hilarity). (AMP)

## Background

Despite the miracles and mercies of God in delivering the children of Israel from Egypt and caring for their many needs, they turned on Moses and God when Moses delayed his return from the Mount. But the crime was not just that they had made a new god, a golden calf, but *they gave thanks to it* for their deliverance from Egypt.

1 And when the people saw that Moses delayed to come down out of the mount, the people

gathered themselves together unto Aaron, and said unto him, Up, **make us gods**, which shall go before us; for as for this Moses, the man that brought us up out of the land of Egypt, we wot not what is become of him.

2 And Aaron said unto them, Break off the golden earrings, which are in the ears of your wives, of your sons, and of your daughters, and bring them unto me.

3 And all the people brake off the golden earrings which were in their ears, and brought them unto Aaron.

4 And he received them at their hand, and fashioned it with a graving tool, after he had made it a **molten calf: and they said, These be thy gods, O Israel, which brought thee up out of the land of Egypt**.

5 And when Aaron saw it, he built an altar before it; and Aaron made proclamation, and said, To morrow is a feast to the Lord.

6 And they rose up early on the morrow, and offered burnt offerings, and brought peace offerings; and the people sat down to eat and to drink, and rose up to play. (Exodus 32)

Under the crime of idolatry are false gods, false belief systems, and false religions.

## FALSE GODS

A "god" is anything that is worshiped. A "false god" is when we worship anything but the true God, which could be vanity and the worship of self and putting of one's *trust* in the "arm of the flesh":

> 5 Thus saith the Lord; **Cursed be the man that trusteth in man, and maketh flesh his arm, and whose heart departeth from the Lord.**
> 7 Blessed is the man that trusteth in the Lord, and whose hope the Lord is. (Jeremiah 17)

What other things might we be placing before God in importance? A religious leader, perhaps like the pope, a prophet, evangelist, healer, guru, or pastor? Or what about the pursuit and accumulation of wealth?

> 10 For **the love of money is the root of all evil**: which while some coveted after, they have erred from the faith, and pierced themselves through with many sorrows. (1 Timothy 6)

Other things we might position over God are pleasures of the flesh, including addictions to food, drugs, sex, music, sports, adrenaline rushes, etc. In short, we should not desire anything on this Earth more than the Creator, and this is the *First and Great Commandment*:

> 37 Jesus said unto him, **Thou shalt love the Lord thy God with all thy heart, and with all thy soul, and with all thy mind.**
> 38 This is the first and great commandment. (Matthew 22)

# FALSE RELIGIONS

Two prophecies confirm false beliefs will be a problem in our time. The first says that Jesus and His *original* Gospel would need to be *sent again*, which supports the premise His Gospel would become *corrupt*.

## Times of Refreshing

> 19 Repent ye therefore, and be converted, that your sins may be blotted out, when the **times of refreshing** shall come from the **presence of the Lord**;
> 20 And **he shall send Jesus Christ, which before was preached unto you:** (Acts 3)

The second prophecy confirms the first and repeats the need for the original, unchangeable, "everlasting" Gospel to be sent—when the "hour of His judgment" has come.

## Everlasting Gospel

> 6 And I saw another angel fly in the midst of Heaven, **having the everlasting gospel to preach** unto them that dwell on the Earth, and to every nation, and kindred, and tongue, and people,
> 7 Saying with a loud voice, Fear God, and give glory to him; for the **hour of his judgment is come:** and worship him that made Heaven,

and Earth, and the sea, and the fountains of waters. (Revelation 14)

As I explain in my title, *Alpha & Omega*, in the first few chapters of *The Revelation of John*, Jesus assessed the condition of seven churches at that time, and according to Him, heresies had already crept in. After two thousand years, one can only imagine how many more errors have become traditional beliefs held by His followers.

25 That **there should be no schism in the body**; but that the members should have the same care one for another. (1 Corinthians 12)

## DON'T BE FORNICATORS

8 **Neither let us commit fornication**, as some of them committed, and fell in one day three and twenty thousand. (1 Corinthians 10)

8 **We should not commit sexual immorality**, as some of them did—and in one day twenty-three thousand of them died. (NIV)

8 And **we must not engage in sexual immorality** as some of them did, causing 23,000 of them to die in one day. (NLT)

8 We **must not gratify evil desire *and* indulge in immorality** as some of them did—and twenty-three thousand [suddenly] fell *dead* in a single day! (AMP)

Bondage | 27

# Background

Many of the men among the children of Israel went whoring after foreign women and bowed down to their gods. They became so bold in their fornications that they brought the women into their tents *in the sight of Moses and the children of Israel* and disgraced themselves.

> 1 And Israel abode in Shittim, and the people **began to commit whoredom with the daughters of Moab.**
> 2 And they called the people unto the sacrifices of their gods: and the people did eat, and bowed down to their gods.
> 3 And Israel joined himself unto Baal-peor: and the anger of the Lord was kindled against Israel.
> 4 And the Lord said unto Moses, Take all the heads of the people, and hang them up before the Lord against the sun, that the fierce anger of the Lord may be turned away from Israel.
> 5 And Moses said unto the judges of Israel, **Slay ye every one his men that were joined unto Baal-peor.**
> 6 And, behold, one of the children of Israel came and brought unto his brethren a Midianitish woman **in the sight of Moses, and in the sight of all the congregation** of the children of Israel, **who were weeping** before the door of the tabernacle of the congregation.
> 7 And when Phinehas, the son of Eleazar, the son of Aaron the priest, saw it, he rose up from

among the congregation, and took a javelin in his hand;

8 And he went after the man of Israel into the tent, and thrust both of them through, the man of Israel, and the woman through her belly. So the plague was stayed from the children of Israel.

9 And **those that died in the plague were twenty and four thousand.** (Numbers 25)

4 The LORD said to Moses, "Take all the leaders of these people, kill them and expose them in broad daylight before the LORD, so that the LORD's fierce anger may turn away from Israel." (NIV) (Numbers 25)

4 The LORD issued the following command to Moses: "Seize all the ringleaders and execute them before the LORD in broad daylight, so his fierce anger will turn away from the people of Israel." (NLT)

4 And the Lord said to Moses, Take all the leaders or chiefs of the people, and hang them before the Lord in the sun [after killing them], that the fierce anger of the Lord may turn away from Israel. (AMP)

4 And Jehovah saith unto Moses, 'Take all the chiefs of the people, and hang them before Jehovah — over-against the sun; and the fierceness of the anger of Jehovah doth turn back from Israel.' (YLT)

That was a great temptation to forsake the living God for the flesh and sex. Even in John's day, Our Lord said they were losing Believers for the same temptation.

> 14 But I have a few things against thee, because thou hast there them that hold the **doctrine of Balaam**, who taught Balac to cast a **stumblingblock before the children of Israel**, to **eat things sacrificed unto idols**, and to **commit fornication**. (Revelation 2)

What appears to be freedom from the rules of morality turns out to be slavery of another kind.

> 19 **While they promise them liberty**, they themselves are the **servants of corruption**: for of whom **a man is overcome**, of the same is he **brought in bondage**.
> 20 For if after they have escaped the pollutions of the world through the knowledge of the Lord and Saviour Jesus Christ, they are again entangled therein, and overcome, **the latter end is worse with them than the beginning**. (2 Peter 2)

## DON'T TEST GOD

> 9 **Neither let us tempt Christ**, as some of them also tempted, and were destroyed of serpents. (1 Corinthians 10)

9 **We should not test Christ**, as some of them did and were killed by snakes. (NIV)

9 **Nor should we put Christ to the test**, as some of them did and then died from snakebites. (NLT)

9 We should not tempt the Lord **[try His patience, become a trial to Him, critically appraise Him, and exploit His goodness]** as some of them did and were killed by poisonous serpents; (AMP)

## Background

Like petulant little children who try their parents' patience, the children of Israel continually tested God's. This time, God responded by killing them with "fiery serpents."

> 5 And **the people spake against God, and against Moses**, Wherefore have ye brought us up out of Egypt to die in the wilderness? for there is no bread, neither is there any water; and our soul loatheth this light bread.
> 6 And the Lord **sent fiery serpents** among the people, and they bit the people; and much people of Israel died.
> 7 Therefore the people came to Moses, and said, **We have sinned, for we have spoken against the Lord**, and against thee; pray unto the Lord, that he take away the serpents from us. (Numbers 21)

# DON'T MURMUR

10 **Neither murmur** ye, as some of them also murmured, and were destroyed of the destroyer. (1 Corinthians 10)

10 And **do not grumble**, as some of them did and were killed by the destroying angel. (NIV)

10 And **don't grumble** as some of them did and were destroyed by the angel of death (NLT)

10 **Nor discontentedly complain** as some of them did and were put out of the way entirely by the destroyer (death). (AMP)

## Background

There were those among the children of Israel who, despite all the good Moses did, still complained, said *they* should be the leaders, and tried to undermine his leadership. These were "men of renown," "famous in the congregation," and "princes of the assembly." Moses had them bring their incense before God, and they would see whose offering God would respect. God did not recognize any of their offerings; they were all swallowed up in the Earth or destroyed with fire.

After all that, some of the people persisted in murmuring against God, so God also destroyed them. In all, God killed nearly 15,000 *men, women, and children* of those who murmured.

1 Now Korah, the son of Izhar, the son of Kohath, the son of Levi, and Dathan and Abiram, the sons of Eliab, and On, the son of Peleth, sons of Reuben, took men:

2 And they rose up before Moses, with certain of the children of Israel, **two hundred and fifty princes of the assembly, famous in the congregation, men of renown**:

3 And they **gathered themselves together against Moses and against Aaron**, and said unto them, Ye take too much upon you, seeing all the congregation are holy, every one of them, and the Lord is among them: **wherefore then lift ye up yourselves above the congregation of the Lord?**

13 Is it a small thing that thou hast brought us up out of a land that floweth with milk and honey, to kill us in the wilderness, except **thou make thyself altogether a prince over us?**

14 Moreover thou hast not brought us into a land that floweth with milk and honey, or given us inheritance of fields and vineyards: wilt thou put out the eyes of these men?

28 And Moses said, Hereby ye shall know that the Lord hath sent me to do all these works; for I have not done them of mine own mind.

29 If these men die the common death of all men, or if they be visited after the visitation of all men; then the Lord hath not sent me.

30 But if the Lord make a new thing, and the Earth open her mouth, and swallow them up, with all that appertain unto them, and they go down quick into the pit; then ye shall under-

stand that these men have provoked the Lord. 31 And it came to pass, as he had made an end of speaking all these words, that the ground clave asunder that was under them:

32 And **the Earth opened her mouth, and swallowed them up, and their houses, and all the men that appertained unto Korah, and all their goods.**

33 They, and all that appertained to them, went down alive into the pit, and the Earth closed upon them: and they perished from among the congregation.

35 And **there came out a fire from the Lord, and consumed the two hundred and fifty men that offered incense.**

41 But on the morrow all the congregation of the children of Israel **murmured against Moses and against Aaron, saying, Ye have killed the people of the Lord.**

49 Now they that died in the **plague** were fourteen thousand and seven hundred, beside them that died about the matter of Korah. (Numbers 16)

## Summary

Paul identified other types of bondage that the children of Israel were under; they are not foreign to us today.

- Don't Crave Carnal Things
- Don't Be Idolaters
- Avoid False Gods

- Avoid False Religions
- Don't Be Fornicators
- Don't Test God
- Don't Murmur

Their story provides a reality check on what human nature is like. Many of those who heard God's voice and saw His glory and power demonstrated turned on Him.

# FEASTS

Undoubtedly, the most familiar *Type* found in the account of Moses and the children of Israel was their *feasts*. I learned a great deal from those and discovered that many Believers already knew that they foreshadowed the Messiah. Some events have already happened depending on whose interpretation you accept, and others will yet occur. God instituted seven feasts (called "Holy Convocations") that the children of Israel were to keep, year after year. They are listed in *Leviticus 23*.

The first three feasts (*Passover, Unleavened Bread, First Fruits*) occur in the Spring, and the last three feasts (*Trumpets, Atonement, Tabernacles*) happen in the Fall, with one in the middle (*Pentecost*). It's clear the first four feasts were fulfilled during the time of Our Lord, and the remaining three Fall Feasts will be fulfilled with His Second Coming.

> The "Feasts of Jehovah" all pointed onward to subjects of eternal interest; subjects on which the mind and heart of God— Father, Son and Holy Spirit— had been engaged before the world was, and which in due time and order, were to take their places in that marvellous chain of events, which when completed, will show the infinite wisdom and love of God, in all His purposes of grace toward the sons of men. They were each a **"shadow of things to**

**come**," of which Christ is the "body" (Col. 2: 16) or substance: foreshadowings of His peerless Person, and infinitely precious work, over which all Believers delight to muse, on which by faith they feed, and which they find to be the strength and joy of their spiritual life.[1]

# TIMING

Because Jesus fulfilled the first four feasts precisely to the day, many believe that the Fall Feasts will follow suit and be fulfilled *to the day*. They theorize that we can know the *day* of Our Lord's coming according to the Feast Days and the *year* according to the Blood Moons. However, that would negate the parables and prophecies Jesus gave, warning us He will come "as a thief in the night," and we need to be watchful at all times, *not just during those Feast Days.*

The following scriptures clarify that Jesus is coming to *harvest* the faithful and innocent. When would be the best time to do that can only be known by God the Father.

> 35 **Say not ye, There are yet four months, and then cometh harvest**? behold, I say unto you, Lift up your eyes, and look on the fields; for **they are white already to harvest**. (John 4)

> 35 Do you not say, '**After four months the harvest comes**?' Behold, I say to you, lift up your eyes and behold the fields that are white and

are **ready to harvest even now**. (John 4 Aramaic in Plain English)

In the parable of The Sower (Mat.13:3-9,18-23) and The Wheat and Tares (Mat.13:24-30), Jesus demonstrates there's a balance between good and evil. At some point, God the Father will initiate His *End Time Sequence* to save as many as possible, including the Earth. When will our "harvest" be ready? Only He knows.

> 14 And I looked, and **behold a white cloud**, and upon the cloud one sat like unto the **Son of man**, having on his head a golden crown, and in his hand a **sharp sickle**.
> 15 And another angel came out of the temple, crying with a loud voice to him that sat on the cloud, **Thrust in thy sickle, and reap**: for the **time is come** for thee to reap; for the **harvest of the Earth is ripe**.
> 16 And he that sat on the cloud thrust in his sickle on the Earth; and the **Earth was reaped**. (Revelation 14)

That prophecy confirms Our Lord will arrive on a "cloud" (with angels on their "clouds") when God says. It may not be on a feast day. Nevertheless, the last three feasts do confirm a *sequence* we can expect.

# PASSOVER

The Passover commemorates God's grace over those houses that had the lamb's blood painted. The angel of death passed by their houses, preserving the lives of their firstborn, while the firstborn in other houses died. This *Type* was fulfilled at the death of Our Lord. A relevance today is that any Believer who lays claim to the blood of Our Lord will not suffer *spiritual* death.

Our "Lord's Supper" fulfilled and replaced Passover observance.

> 4 These are the feasts of the Lord, even holy convocations, which ye shall proclaim in their seasons.
> 5 In the fourteenth day of the first month at even is the **Lord's passover**. (Lev. 23)

> 7 Purge out therefore the old leaven, that ye may be a new lump, as ye are unleavened. For even **Christ our passover** is sacrificed for us. (1 Corinthians 5)

> 26 And as they were eating, Jesus took bread, and blessed it, and brake it, and gave it to the disciples, and said, Take, eat; this is my body.
> 27 And he took the cup, and gave thanks, and gave it to them, saying, Drink ye all of it;
> 28 For this is my blood of the new testament, which is shed for many for the remission of sins. (Matthew 26)

23 For I have received of the Lord that which also I delivered unto you, That the Lord Jesus the same night in which he was betrayed took bread:
24 And when he had given thanks, he brake it, and said, Take, eat: this is my body, which is broken for you: this do in remembrance of me.
25 After the same manner also he took the cup, when he had supped, saying, This cup is the **new testament in my blood**: this do ye, as oft as ye drink it, in remembrance of me.
26 For as often as ye eat this bread, and drink this cup, **ye do shew the Lord's death till he come**. (1 Corinthians 11)

## FEAST OF UNLEAVENED BREAD

This is the second of three Pilgrimage Feasts (Deut. 16:16) that required all males to attend in Jerusalem, which was fulfilled when Our Lord was placed in the tomb.

> 6 And on the fifteenth day of the same [first] month is the **feast of unleavened bread** unto the Lord: seven days ye must eat unleavened bread.
> 7 In the first day ye shall have an holy convocation: ye shall do no servile work therein.
> 8 But ye shall offer an offering made by fire unto the Lord seven days: in the seventh day is an holy convocation: ye shall do no servile work therein. (Lev. 23)

How this was fulfilled:

> The feast of unleavened bread began on the day after the Passover and continued for seven days, a perfect period of time. The lamb was slain on the fourteenth day, at sunset; the feast of unleavened bread began immediately after the fifteenth day commenced, which was just after sunset, so that there would be really no lapse of time between, **no interval between the death of the lamb, the sprinkling of the blood**, and the keeping of the feast. And thus it was when the feast was first kept in the land of Egypt. The lamb was slain in the evening, the judgment fell at midnight, and the redeemed of the Lord were out of Egypt in the morning.[2]

## FEAST OF FIRSTFRUITS

Firstfruits is also called *Reishit*. This feast was fulfilled when Our Lord rose from the dead as the "first fruits" of the resurrected.

> 9 And the Lord spake unto Moses, saying,
> 10 Speak unto the children of Israel, and say unto them, When ye be come into the land which I give unto you, and shall reap the harvest thereof, then ye shall bring a sheaf of the firstfruits of your harvest unto the priest:
> 11 And he shall wave the sheaf before the Lord, to be accepted for you: on the morrow after the sabbath the priest shall wave it.
> 12 And ye shall offer that day when ye wave the

sheaf an he **lamb without blemish** of the first year for a burnt offering unto the Lord.

13 And the meat offering thereof shall be two tenth deals of fine flour mingled with oil, an offering made by fire unto the Lord for a sweet savour: and the drink offering thereof shall be of wine, the fourth part of an hin.

14 And ye shall eat neither bread, nor parched corn, nor green ears, until the selfsame day that ye have brought an offering unto your God: **it shall be a statute for ever throughout your generations** in all your dwellings. (Lev. 23)

## PENTECOST

This feast is called *Shavuot*, the *Feast of Weeks* and *Feast of Harvest*. It comes 50 *days* after Passover, is a Pilgrimage Feast, and was fulfilled on Pentecost after Our Lord rose from the dead. It's when the Holy Spirit was poured out upon the apostles.

15 And ye shall count unto you from the morrow after the sabbath, from the day that ye brought the sheaf of the wave offering; seven sabbaths shall be complete:

16 Even unto the morrow after the seventh sabbath shall ye number **fifty days**; and ye shall offer a new meat offering unto the Lord.

17 Ye shall bring out of your habitations two wave loaves of two tenth deals: they shall be of fine flour; they shall be baken with leaven; they are the firstfruits unto the Lord.

18 And ye shall offer with the bread seven lambs without blemish of the first year, and one young bullock, and two rams: they shall be for a burnt offering unto the Lord, with their meat offering, and their drink offerings, even **an offering made by fire**, of sweet savour unto the Lord.
19 Then ye shall sacrifice one kid of the goats for a sin offering, and two lambs of the first year for a sacrifice of peace offerings.
20 And the priest shall wave them with the bread of the firstfruits for a wave offering before the Lord, with the two lambs: they shall be holy to the Lord for the priest.
21 And ye shall proclaim on the selfsame day, that it may be an **holy convocation unto you**: ye shall do no servile work therein: it shall be a statute for ever in all your dwellings throughout your generations.
22 And when ye reap the harvest of your land, thou shalt not make clean riddance of the corners of thy field when thou reapest, neither shalt thou gather any gleaning of thy harvest: thou shalt leave them unto the poor, and to the stranger: I am the Lord your God. (Lev. 23)

## FEAST OF TRUMPETS

It is also called *Rosh Hashanah* by modern Jews and is the *New Year*. The shofar is blown 100 *times*.

23 And the Lord spake unto Moses, saying,
24 Speak unto the children of Israel, saying,

> In the seventh month, in the first day of the month, shall ye have a sabbath, a memorial of **blowing of trumpets**, an holy convocation.
> 25 Ye shall do no servile work therein: but ye shall offer an offering made by fire unto the Lord. (Lev. 23)

This coincides with Our Lord's appearance, for according to the prophecies, trumpets will accompany Him.

> 16 For the Lord himself shall descend from Heaven with a shout, with the voice of the archangel, and with the **trump of God**: and the dead in Christ shall rise first:
> 17 Then we which are alive and remain shall be caught up together with them in the clouds, to meet the Lord in the air: and so shall we ever be with the Lord. (1 Thessalonians 4)

> 51 Behold, I shew you a mystery; We shall not all sleep, but we shall all be changed,
> 52 In a moment, in the twinkling of an eye, at the last trump: **for the trumpet shall sound**, and the dead shall be raised incorruptible, and we shall be changed. (1 Corinthians 15)

Additional quotes:

> **The trumpet was the signal for the field workers to come into the Temple.** The high priest actually stood on the southwestern parapet of the Temple and blew the trumpet so that it could be heard in the surrounding

fields. **At that instant, the faithful would stop harvesting** even if there were more crops to bring in, and leave immediately for the worship services.[3]

Today is the birthday of the world; today **God will sit in judgment over all the world's creations** (from the Rosh Hashana mussaf service). Rosh Hashana is a day on which each person individually, and the nations of the world collectively, are judged by an omniscient, omnipotent God.[4]

On Rosh Hashana Jews commemorate God's creation of the world. He alone created; He alone commands the Earth below and the sky above. **Rosh Hashana is the annual coronation of the King of Kings**, a ceremony glorified by the Jewish people's observance of it. Both the liturgy and the festive meal demonstrate and celebrate our acceptance of God as the ultimate ruler. This absolute sovereign, however, is also the supreme judge. Rosh Hashana combines two related themes: It celebrates the dominion of the King of Kings, the mighty God of the Jewish people, while it instills the **awe and fear that people must feel before the king pronounces judgment over his subjects.**[5]

To elicit both divine dominion and mercy, the ram's horn – the shofar – is sounded. The blowing of the shofar is the only specific commandment for Rosh Hashana. The shofar is recognized as the Rosh Hashana symbol by all ages of people, and a most fitting symbol it

*Feasts* | 45

is, for its one hundred blasts nobly suggest and reinforce the day's dual theme. Just as trumpeters **announce the presence of a mortal king**, Jews proclaim the **coronation of the King of Kings**. Yet, the shofar also promotes introspection; each loud, simple blast **reminds one of imminent divine judgment**. The ram's horn is an especially appropriate symbol, for it reminds the Jewish people as well as the Almighty of Abraham's willingness to sacrifice his son Isaac, to fulfill God's command. **At the very last second**, God ordered Abraham to replace Isaac with a sacrificial ram. The Torah reading for the second day of Rosh Hashana is 'The Sacrifice of Isaac' (Gen. 22), again recalling the patriarch's absolute devotion.[6]

## DAY OF ATONEMENT

It is also called *Yom Kippur* and *Days of Repentance*. It's the most solemn day of the Feasts. There's a *ten-day waiting period* between Rosh Hashanah and Yom Kippur called *Days of Awe*, and it is spent repenting to try and change God's mind about the outcome. Typically, one would associate Our Lord's sacrifice with the Atonement, but since it has already been tied to the Passover, the meaning of the *Day of Atonement* must be found elsewhere. It's not about the Messiah atoning anymore; *it's about us receiving it* by afflicting our souls *through repentance*.

Note in the following stanza that people who do not humble themselves will be cut off.

26 And the Lord spake unto Moses, saying,
27 Also on the tenth day of this seventh month there shall be a **day of atonement**: it shall be an holy convocation unto you; and ye shall **afflict your souls**, and offer an offering made by fire unto the Lord.
28 And ye shall do no work in that same day: for it is a **day of atonement**, to make an atonement for you before the Lord your God.
29 **For whatsoever soul it be that shall not be afflicted in that same day, he shall be cut off from among his people**.
30 And whatsoever soul it be that doeth any work in that same day, the same soul will I destroy from among his people.
31 Ye shall do no manner of work: it shall be a statute for ever throughout your generations in all your dwellings.
32 It shall be unto you a sabbath of rest, and **ye shall afflict your souls**: in the ninth day of the month at even, from even unto even, shall ye celebrate your sabbath. (Lev. 23)

Additional quotes:

According to Jewish tradition, God inscribes each person's fate for the coming year into a book, the Book of Life, on Rosh Hashanah, and **waits until Yom Kippur to "seal" the verdict**. During the Days of Awe, a Jew **tries to amend his or her behavior and seek forgive-**

ness for wrongs done against God** (bein adam leMakom) and against other human beings (bein adam lechavero). The evening and day of Yom Kippur are set aside for public and private petitions and confessions of guilt (Vidui). At the end of Yom Kippur, **one hopes that they have been forgiven by God.**[7]

A preliminary judgment will be made on Yom Kippur.

> One of the ongoing themes of the *Days of Awe* is the concept that G-d has 'books' that he writes our names in, writing down who will live and who will die, who will have a good life and who will have a bad life, for the next year. **These books are written in on Rosh Hashanah, but our actions during the *Days of Awe* can alter G-d's decree**. The actions that change the decree are 'teshuvah, tefilah and tzedakah,' repentance, prayer, good deeds (usually, charity). These 'books' are sealed on *Yom Kippur*. This concept of writing in books is the source of the common greeting during this time is 'May you be inscribed and sealed for a good year.'
>
> Among the customs of this time, it is common to seek reconciliation with people you may have wronged during the course of the year. The *Talmud* maintains that *Yom Kippur* atones only for sins between man and G-d. To atone for sins against another person, you must first seek reconciliation with that per-

son, righting the wrongs you committed against them if possible.[8]

God, in His infinite mercy, is planning to humble us to save us.

> 11 The **lofty looks of man shall be humbled**, and the haughtiness of men shall be bowed down, and the Lord alone shall be exalted in that day.
> 12 For **the day of the Lord of hosts shall be upon every one that is proud** and lofty, and upon every one that is lifted up; and he shall be brought low:
> 13 And upon all the cedars of Lebanon, that are high and lifted up, and upon all the oaks of Bashan,
> 14 And upon all the high mountains, and upon all the hills that are lifted up,
> 15 And upon every high tower, and upon every fenced wall,
> 16 And upon all the ships of Tarshish, and upon all pleasant pictures.
> 17 And **the loftiness of man shall be bowed down, and the haughtiness of men shall be made low: and the Lord alone shall be exalted in that day**. (Isaiah 2)

One of the ways He will humble us will be through the "shaking" of the Heavens and the Earth, literally or figuratively.

> 19 for fear of the Lord, and for **the glory of his majesty**, when he **ariseth to shake terri-**

**bly the Earth**.
21 for fear of the Lord, and for **the glory of his majesty**, when he **ariseth to shake terribly the Earth**. (Isaiah 2)

## FEAST OF TABERNACLES

It is also called *Sukkot* or *Feast of Booths* and commemorates the 40-year wilderness journey by the children of Israel when they dwelt in "booths." Modern observers do the same for the same length of time.

> 33 And the Lord spake unto Moses, saying,
> 34 Speak unto the children of Israel, saying, The fifteenth day of this seventh month shall be the **feast of tabernacles** for seven days unto the Lord.
> 35 On the first day shall be an holy convocation: ye shall do no servile work therein.
> 36 **Seven days** ye shall offer an offering made by fire unto the Lord: on the eighth day shall be an holy convocation unto you; and ye shall offer an offering made by fire unto the Lord: it is a solemn assembly; and ye shall do no servile work therein.
> 37 These are the feasts of the Lord, which ye shall proclaim to be holy convocations, to offer an offering made by fire unto the Lord, a burnt offering, and a meat offering, a sacrifice, and drink offerings, every thing upon his day:
> 38 Beside the sabbaths of the Lord, and beside your gifts, and beside all your vows, and

beside all your freewill offerings, which ye give unto the Lord.

39 Also in the fifteenth day of the seventh month, when ye have gathered in the fruit of the land, ye shall keep a feast unto the Lord seven days: on the first day shall be a sabbath, and on the eighth day shall be a sabbath.

40 And ye shall take you on the first day the boughs of goodly trees, branches of palm trees, and the boughs of thick trees, and willows of the brook; and ye shall rejoice before the Lord your God seven days.

41 And ye shall keep it a feast unto the Lord seven days in the year. It shall be a statute for ever in your generations: ye shall celebrate it in the seventh month.

42 **Ye shall dwell in booths seven days**; all that are Israelites born shall dwell in booths:

43 That your generations may know that I made the children of Israel to dwell in booths, when I brought them out of the land of Egypt: I am the Lord your God.

44 And Moses declared unto the children of Israel the feasts of the Lord. (Leviticus 23)

It also celebrates the *Fall Harvest* and is a Pilgrimage Feast. Some believe Sukkot will continue to be celebrated *in Jerusalem* through The Millennium.

16 And it shall come to pass, that every one that is left of all the nations which came against Jerusalem **shall even go up from year to year to worship the King, the Lord of**

> **hosts**, and to **keep the feast of tabernacles**.
> 17 And it shall be, that whoso will not come up of all the families of the earth unto Jerusalem to worship the King, the Lord of hosts, even upon them shall be no rain.
> 18 And if the family of Egypt go not up, and come not, that have no rain; there shall be the plague, wherewith the Lord will smite the heathen that come not up to keep the feast of tabernacles.
> 19 This shall be the punishment of Egypt, and the punishment of all nations that come not up to keep the **feast of tabernacles**. (Zechariah 14)

Christians may understand this to be fulfilled when the New Jerusalem arrives. It portends to the time when *God's tabernacle* dwells "with man":

> 1 And I saw a new Heaven and a new Earth: for the first Heaven and the first Earth were passed away; and there was no more sea.
> 2 And I John saw the **holy city, new Jerusalem, coming down from God out of Heaven**, prepared as a bride adorned for her husband.
> 3 And I heard a great voice out of Heaven saying, **Behold, the tabernacle of God is with men**, and he will dwell with them, and they shall be his people, and God himself shall be with them, and be their God. (Revelation 21)

Notice that John saw it "coming down," but not on

the Earth. When it becomes visible to us, it will be considered *with* humanity.

## SUMMARY

- *Passover* = Jesus died
- *Unleavened Bread* = Jesus buried
- *First Fruits* = Jesus rose
- *Pentecost* = Spirit poured out
- *Trumpets* = The Sign of Jesus' Coming
- *Atonement* = A time to repent
- *Tabernacles* = The New Jerusalem Arrives

Notes

1. John Ritchie, *Feasts of Jehovah: Foreshadows of Christ in the Calendar of Israel.*
2. Ibid.
3. Zola Levitt, *The Seven Feasts of Israel.*
4. *Celebration, the Book of Jewish Festivals,* 1987, p. 10.
5. Ibid.
6. Ibid.
7. Wikipedia—*Day of Atonement.*
8. *Jewish Virtual Library.*

# DARKNESS

The scriptures speak of darkness in many forms, including physical, mental, emotional, and spiritual. The darkness the children of Israel experienced was emotional and spiritual, and the form the armies of Pharaoh experienced was physical. These *Types* have relevance to us in these last days where it was already prophesied that extreme darkness would cover the Earth.

> 2 For, behold, the **darkness shall cover the earth**, and **GROSS DARKNESS the people**: but the LORD shall arise upon thee, and his glory shall be seen upon thee. (Isaiah 60)

After Moses and the children of Israel had left Egypt, Pharaoh's heart had become hardened yet again, and he still pursued after them. According to Josephus, *fifty thousand horsemen* and *two hundred thousand footmen* were pursuing some two million Hebrews.[1]

The account of Moses makes it clear they were "cornered" or "shut in" with nowhere to go, and when they saw Pharaoh's armies approach, their hearts dropped, and they were engulfed in *fear* (emotional darkness).

> 8 And the **LORD hardened the heart of Pharaoh king of Egypt**, and he **pursued after the children of Israel**: and the children of

Israel went out with an high hand.
9 But the Egyptians pursued after them, all the **horses** and **chariots** of Pharaoh, and his **horsemen,** and his **army,** and overtook them encamping by the sea, beside Pihahiroth, before Baalzephon.
10 And when Pharaoh drew nigh, the **children of Israel lifted up their eyes**, and, behold, the Egyptians marched after them; and **they were SORE AFRAID**: and the **CHILDREN OF ISRAEL CRIED OUT UNTO THE LORD.**
11 And they said unto Moses, Because there were no graves in Egypt, **hast thou taken us away to die in the wilderness?** wherefore hast thou dealt thus with us, to carry us forth out of Egypt? (Exodus 14)

To buy time, the angel of the Lord went between them and appeared as a "cloud of darkness" to the Egyptians.

19 And the angel of God, which went before the camp of Israel, removed and went behind them; and the pillar of the cloud went from before their face, and stood behind them:
20 And it **came between the camp of the Egyptians and the camp of Israel**; and it was **a CLOUD and DARKNESS [physical darkness]** to them, but it gave light by night to these: so that the one came not near the other all the night.
21 And Moses stretched out his hand over the sea; and the Lord caused the sea to go back

by a strong east wind all that night, and made the sea dry land, and the waters were divided. (Exodus 14)

The darkness they experienced is a *Type* we will encounter before Our Lord returns—both the spiritual and the physical.

1 Blow ye the trumpet in Zion, and sound an alarm in my holy mountain: let all the inhabitants of the land tremble: for the day of the Lord cometh, for it is nigh at hand;
2 **A day of DARKNESS and of gloominess, a day of CLOUDS and of THICK DARKNESS,** as the morning spread upon the mountains: **a great people and a strong**; there hath not been ever the like, neither shall be any more after it, even to the years of many generations. (Joel 2)

18 **Woe unto you that desire the DAY OF THE LORD!** to what end is it for you? **the DAY OF THE LORD is DARKNESS, and not light.**
19 As if a man did flee from a lion, and a bear met him; or went into the house, and leaned his hand on the wall, and a serpent bit him.
20 **Shall not the DAY OF THE LORD be DARKNESS, and not light? even VERY DARK, and no brightness in it?** (Amos 5)

14 The **GREAT DAY OF THE LORD** is near, it is near, and hasteth greatly, even the voice of the **DAY OF THE LORD**: the mighty man shall cry there bitterly.

15 That day is a day of wrath, a day of trouble and distress, a day of wasteness and desolation, **a DAY of DARKNESS and GLOOMINESS, a day of CLOUDS and THICK DARKNESS.** (Zephaniah 1)

The coming Antichrist threatens to engulf humanity in an environment where the people will feel they "must" take the Mark of the Beast (Rev.13:17, 15:2). The fear caused by the threat of "going without" (i.e., can't buy or sell) unless we take its mark in an age of convenience could, for many, be an equal threat to what the children of Israel felt when they found themselves hemmed in with no place to go.

The lesson we can learn from this *Type* is when we feel hemmed in by our situation—be it the Mark of the Beast or another—we must TURN TO GOD and cry out with all our might as did the children of Israel and wait for Him to act.

Notes

1. Josephus, *Antiquities of the Jews*, Bk II, Ch. XV.

# WATERS DIVIDED

The dividing of the *Red Sea* is another *Type* of an incredible event prophesied to happen in our day.

> 21 And Moses stretched out his hand over the sea; and the Lord caused the sea to go back by a strong east wind all that night, and made the sea dry land, and the **waters were divided**. (Exodus 14)

I liken that to the prophecy of the "heavens splitting" or our sky parting, like when a scroll is rolled up, and you no longer see the usual contents you're accustomed to viewing.

> 4 And all the host of heaven shall be dissolved, and the **heavens shall be rolled together as a scroll**: and all their host shall fall down, as the leaf falleth off from the vine, and as a falling fig from the fig tree. (Isaiah 34)

> 12 And I beheld **when he had opened the sixth seal**, and, lo, there was a great earthquake; and the sun became black as sackcloth of hair, and the moon became as blood;
> 13 And the stars of Heaven fell unto the Earth, even as a fig tree casteth her untimely figs, when she is shaken of a mighty wind.
> 14 And **the Heaven *departed* as a scroll** when it is rolled together; and every mountain and island were moved out of their places.

15 And the kings of the Earth, and the great men, and the rich men, and the chief captains, and the mighty men, and every bondman, and every free man, hid themselves in the dens and in the rocks of the mountains;
16 And said to the mountains and rocks, Fall on us, and hide us from the face of him that sitteth on the throne, and from the wrath of the Lamb:
17 For the great day of his wrath is come; and who shall be able to stand? (Revelation 6)

A *spiritual unveiling* may come—something akin to a *dimensional shift*—before a physical one occurs.

# SPLIT ROCK

*Rock of Horeb, ©Ross Patterson*

The story of Moses splitting a rock in Horeb that gushed forth water for the children of Israel and their animals is a significant *Type*.

> 6 Behold, I will stand before thee there upon the **rock in Horeb**; and thou shalt **smite the rock**, and there shall **come water out of it**, that the people may drink. And Moses did so in the sight of the elders of Israel. (Exodus 17)

> 15 He **clave [split] the rocks** in the wilderness, and gave them drink as out of the great depths.
> 16 He brought streams also out of the rock,

and **caused waters to run down like rivers**. (Psalms 78)

21 And they thirsted not when he led them through the deserts: he caused the waters to flow out of the rock for them: **he clave [split] the rock** also, and the **waters gushed out**. (Isaiah 48)

Keep in mind God did not need to split a rock in order to bring forth water. This was purely a symbolic gesture for something in the future: a *Type*.

That future event was not known with certainty in the first edition of this book, but it has now been identified as mentioned in the *Preface* and a book written about it.

For additional pictures and information, see Chapter *Signs & Wonders* in the section "Dr. David Kim."

For what is significant about this *Type*, see Chapter *Vision*.

TESTIMONY: *Temple Mount 11:11 Horn of God* EXPANDED

# FIERY SERPENT

*Elevation of the Brazen Serpent, Willem van den Broecke, 1563*

Another *Type* with more than one meaning is the Fiery Serpent, which most people associate with Our Lord's first coming when He was lifted up on the cross. Here's the backstory on the fiery serpents.

After everything God did to deliver the children of Israel from Pharoah, they began to murmur against Him, so He sent fiery serpents to sting them, and they began to die. At some point, the people realized the reason for this plague and asked for forgiveness.

God gave it through a *symbolic* act of looking

up at a fiery serpent lifted on a pole. The children of Israel needed to simply look upon it to receive relief.

> 5 And the **people spake against God**, and **against Moses**, Wherefore have ye brought us up out of Egypt to die in the wilderness? for there is no bread, neither is there any water; and our soul loatheth this light bread.
> 6 And the Lord sent **fiery serpents** among the people, and they bit the people; and **much people of Israel died**.
> 7 Therefore the people came to Moses, and said, We have sinned, for we have **spoken against the Lord**, and **against thee**; pray unto the Lord, that he take away the serpents from us. And **Moses prayed for the people**.
> 8 And the Lord said unto Moses, **Make thee a fiery serpent, and set it upon a pole**: and it shall come to pass, that **every one that is bitten, when he looketh upon it, shall live**. (Numbers 21)

The analogy is evident concerning Our Lord's first coming when He was lifted on a cross.

> 13 And no man hath **ascended up to Heaven**, but he that came down from Heaven, even the Son of man which is in Heaven.
> 14 And **as Moses lifted up the serpent in the wilderness, even so must the Son of man be lifted up**:

> 15 That **whosoever believeth in him should not perish,** but have eternal life. (John 3)
>
> 32 And I, **if I be lifted up from the Earth, will draw all men unto me.** (John 12)

Another meaning could be derived from the *Second Coming* of Our Lord and the return of The Holy Shekinah. The "fiery serpents" could represent The Holy Shekinah, the light of which is like a fire that cuts to the souls of the wicked, compelling them to repent or suffer their fate—the *Second Death*—for rejecting the Lord Jesus.

> 11 He that hath an ear, let him hear what the Spirit saith unto the churches; **He that overcometh shall not be hurt of the SECOND DEATH.** (Revelation 2)
>
> 6 Blessed and holy is he that hath part in the first resurrection: **on such the SECOND DEATH hath no power**, but they shall be priests of God and of Christ, and shall reign with him a thousand years. (Revelation 20)
>
> 8 **But the fearful, and unbelieving, and the abominable, and murderers, and whoremongers, and sorcerers, and idolaters, and all liars, shall have their part in the lake which burneth with fire and brimstone: which is the SECOND DEATH.** (Revelation 21)

The cure will be the same as it was for the children of Israel; all they need do is look at The Shekinah with *acceptance* and be *saved*. The main similarity is the speed by which relief (Salvation) will come, saving them from the Second Death.

21 And it shall come to pass, that **WHOSOEVER shall CALL on the name of the Lord shall be SAVED**. (Acts 2)

13 For **WHOSOEVER shall CALL upon the name of the Lord shall be SAVED**. (Romans 10)

30 And brought them out, and said, Sirs, **what must I do to be SAVED**?
31 And they said, **BELIEVE on the Lord Jesus Christ**, and thou shalt be saved, and thy house. (Acts 16)

8 For **by GRACE are ye saved through FAITH**; and that not of yourselves: **it is the GIFT of GOD** (Ephesians 2)

9 For God hath not appointed us to wrath, but to **obtain SALVATION by our Lord Jesus Christ**,
10 Who died for us, that, whether we wake or sleep, **we should live together with him**. (1 Thessalonians 5)

23 Then said one unto him, Lord, **are there few that be SAVED**? And he said unto them,
24 Strive to enter in at the strait gate: for many, I say unto you, will seek to enter in, and **shall not be able**. (Luke 13)

> 17 For God sent not his Son into the world to condemn the world; but that **the world through him might be SAVED.**
> 18 **He that BELIEVETH on him is NOT CONDEMNED:** but he that believeth not is condemned already, because he hath not believed in the name of the only begotten Son of God.
> 19 And this is the condemnation, that **LIGHT IS COME** into the world, and **men loved darkness rather than light, because their deeds were evil.**
> 20 For **every one that doeth evil HATETH the LIGHT, NEITHER COMETH TO THE LIGHT, lest his deeds should be reproved.**
> 21 But he that doeth truth **COMETH TO THE LIGHT**, that his deeds may be made manifest, that they are wrought in God. (John 3)

Don't be like "Doubting Thomas," and disbelieve in Our Lord until you see proof; in this case, The Shekinah.

> 29 Jesus saith unto him, **Thomas,** because thou hast seen me, thou hast believed: **blessed are they that have not seen, and yet have believed.** (John 20)

Know that He is real. Trust the Holy Records. Listen to and respect the testimonies of others, and most of all, listen to the conscience God has placed inside of you.

# EAGLES' WINGS

Two *Types* relate to *The Rapture*. For those not familiar with The Rapture, it's the belief that the faithful will be "taken up" from the Earth in the Last Days to escape a *Tribulation* brought on by the *Antichrist*. Here are some background verses.

> 14 And he said to me, These are they which **came out of great TRIBULATION,** and have washed their robes, and made them white in the blood of the Lamb. (Revelation 7)

> 35 For **as a SNARE shall it come on all them that dwell on the face of the whole earth**.
> 36 Watch ye therefore, and pray always, that ye may be accounted **worthy to ESCAPE** all these things that shall come to pass, **and to stand before the Son of man**. (Luke 21)

> 16 And he causeth all, both small and great, rich and poor, free and bond, **to RECEIVE a MARK in their right hand, or in their foreheads**:
> 17 And that no man might buy or sell, save he that had the mark, or the name of the beast, or the number of his name.
> 18 Here is wisdom. Let him that hath understanding count the number of the beast: for it is the number of a man; and his number is **Six hundred threescore and six**. (Revelation 13)

9 And the third angel followed them, saying with a loud voice, **If any man worship the BEAST** and **his IMAGE,** and **receive his MARK in his forehead, or in his hand**,
10 The same shall **drink of the wine of the wrath of God**, which is poured out without mixture into the cup of his indignation; and **he shall be tormented with fire and brimstone in the presence of the holy angels, and in the presence of the Lamb**:
11 And the smoke of their **torment** ascendeth up **for ever and ever: and they have no rest day nor night**, who worship the beast and his image, and whosoever receiveth the mark of his name. (Revelation 14)

14 And I looked, and behold **a WHITE CLOUD**, and upon the cloud one **sat** like unto the **SON OF MAN [JESUS]**, having on his head a golden crown, and in his hand **a sharp sickle**.
15 And another angel came out of the temple, crying with a loud voice to him that sat on the cloud, **Thrust in thy sickle, and REAP [RAPTURE]**: for the time is come for thee to reap; for the harvest of the earth is ripe.
16 And he that sat on the cloud thrust in his sickle on the earth; and **the EARTH WAS REAPED**. (Revelation 14)

The first *Type* related to The Rapture from the account of Moses and the children of Israel is *Pharoah*. Pharoah is the Antichrist *Type* who relentlessly pursues the children of Israel with his army. The Antichrist will *relentlessly* pursue Christians who refuse the Beast System.

> 9 But **the Egyptians PURSUED after them**, all the **horses** and **chariots of PHARAOH,** and his **horsemen,** and his **ARMY,** and overtook them encamping by the sea, beside Pi-hahiroth, before Baal-zephon. (Exodus 14)

The second *Type* related to The Rapture is "Eagles' Wings." This is how it says the children of Israel were delivered from Pharaoh's army:

> 4 Ye have seen what I did unto the Egyptians, and how **I BARE YOU ON EAGLES' WINGS**, and **brought you** UNTO MYSELF. (Exodus 19)

We, too, will escape our future enemy (the Antichrist) on *Eagles' Wings* and be brought to God.

> 13 And when the **dragon** saw that he was **cast unto the Earth** [has not happened yet], he persecuted the **WOMAN [CHRISTIANS/ JEWS]** which brought forth the man child.
> 14 And to the **woman [faithful Christians/ Jews]** were given **TWO WINGS OF A GREAT EAGLE**, that she might fly into the **WILDERNESS [HEAVEN]**, into her place, where she is nourished for a time, and times, and half a time, from the face of the serpent. (Revelation 12)

The following verse is not usually considered a

*Eagles' Wings*

Rapture verse, but in light of the above, it very well may become one.

> 31 But they that **WAIT UPON THE LORD** shall renew their strength; **they shall mount up with WINGS AS EAGLES**; they shall run, and not be weary; and they shall walk, and not faint. (Isaiah 40)

This following prophecy undoubtedly points to a Rapture.

> 27 For just as lightning goes out from The East and appears unto The West, so will the **COMING OF THE SON OF MAN** be.
> 28 Wherever the body will be, **there will the EAGLES [FAITHFUL] BE GATHERED.** (Matthew 24 Aramaic in Plain English)

Their gathering will be celebrated at the "Marriage Supper of the Lamb."

> 7 Let us be glad and rejoice, and give honour to him: for the **MARRIAGE of the LAMB is come**, and his wife hath made herself ready.
> 8 And to her was granted that she should be arrayed in fine linen, clean and white: for the **fine linen is the RIGHTEOUSNESS of [RAPTURED] SAINTS.**
> 9 And he saith unto me, Write, **Blessed are they which are called unto the MARRIAGE SUPPER OF THE LAMB.** And he saith unto me, These are the true sayings of God. (Revelation 19)

# LANDS OF PROMISE

The account of Moses and the children of Israel is a shadow of what we can expect to happen in the *Final Days* on Earth. The final event for the children of Israel was entering their Lands of Promise—*Canaan*. For us, it will be coming to the Marriage Supper of the Lamb, then back to Earth to inherit our own Lands of Promise, where we will *live* and *reign* with Christ through *The Millennium of Peace*.

> 9 And they sung a new song, saying, Thou art worthy to take the book, and to open the seals thereof: for thou wast slain, and **hast redeemed us to God** by thy blood out of every kindred, and tongue, and people, and nation; 10 And **hast made us unto our God KINGS and PRIESTS: and we shall REIGN on the EARTH.** (Revelation 5)

> 6 Blessed and holy is he that hath part in the first resurrection: on such the second death hath no power, but **they shall be PRIESTS of GOD and of CHRIST, and shall REIGN WITH HIM A THOUSAND YEARS.** (Revelation 20)

A review of the account of the children of Israel entering, or not entering, their Lands of Promise will help us know how we can prepare to enter our own successfully.

# THEIR LANDS OF PROMISE

God told Moses He had a land for the children of Israel that was flowing with milk and honey.

> 7 And the Lord said, I have surely seen the affliction of my people which are in Egypt, and have heard their cry by reason of their taskmasters; for I know their sorrows;
> 8 And I am come down to deliver them out of the hand of the Egyptians, and to bring them up out of that land **unto a good land and a large, unto a land flowing with milk and honey;** (Exodus 3)

## Not Everyone Entered

Not all of the children of Israel made it into their Lands of Promise. God cursed some for murmuring, being ungrateful, lacking faith, and for acts of disrespect. Some of the children of Israel died of natural causes during their 40-year expulsion in the wilderness.

The reasons why they did not make it in may become the same reasons why our modern people don't make it into theirs.

## Background

As the children of Israel approached their Lands of Promise, God had Moses send out the heads of each of the Twelve Tribes to scout their lands.

> 2 **Send thou men, that they may search the land of Canaan,** which I give unto the children of Israel: of every tribe of their fathers shall ye send a man, every one a ruler among them. (Numbers 13)

Ten of those twelve leaders returned and gave *unfavorable* reports.

> 32 And they **brought up an EVIL REPORT of the land** which they had searched unto the children of Israel (Numbers 13)

Those reports and leaders caused the children of Israel to *turn against God*, His promises, Moses, and their blessed lands.

> 1 And all the congregation lifted up their voice, and cried; and the people wept that night.
> 2 And **ALL the CHILDREN of ISRAEL MURMURED** against Moses and against Aaron: and the whole congregation said unto them, **Would God that we had died in the land of Egypt! or would God we had died in this wilderness!** (Numbers 14)

Because of this, those ten leaders were cursed by God and died.

> 37 Even those men that did bring up the evil report upon the land, **died by the plague before the Lord.** (Numbers 14)

## Died In The Wilderness

The children of Israel who believed their negative reports and were swayed from following God would not be allowed to enter their Lands of Promise either. But instead of being cursed to death, they had to wander in the wilderness for forty years until everyone over the age of twenty was dead.

> 26 And the Lord spake unto Moses and unto Aaron, saying,
> 27 How long shall I bear with this evil congregation, which murmur against me? I have heard the murmurings of the children of Israel, which they murmur against me.
> 28 Say unto them, As truly as I live, saith the Lord, as ye have spoken in mine ears, so will I do to you:
> 29 **Your carcases shall fall in this wilderness;** and all that were numbered of you, according to your whole number, **from twenty years old and upward,** which have murmured against me,
> 33 And **your children shall wander in the wilderness forty years,** and bear your whoredoms, until your carcases be wasted in the wilderness.
> 34 After the number of the days in which ye searched the land, even forty days, each day for a year, shall ye bear your iniquities, even forty years, and ye shall know my breach of promise.

35 I the Lord have said, **I will surely do it unto all this evil congregation, that are gathered together against me:** in this wilderness they shall be consumed, and there they shall die. (Numbers 14)

## Why They Did Not Enter

What can we learn from those who did not enter their Lands of Promise? Why were they not allowed to enter? As we just read, the leaders gave a bad report that contradicted God, and then they used their influence to sway others. What did their reports say? They said that the current inhabitants of those lands were *too big (giants)*, and their cities were *too fortified (walled)*.

> 25 And they returned from searching of the land after forty days.
> 26 And they went and came to Moses, and to Aaron, and to all the congregation of the children of Israel, unto the wilderness of Paran, to Kadesh; and brought back word unto them, and unto all the congregation, and shewed them the fruit of the land.
> 27 And they told him, and said, We came unto the land whither thou sentest us, and surely it floweth with milk and honey; and this is the fruit of it.
> 28 Nevertheless the **people be strong that dwell in the land,** and the **cities are walled, and very great:** and moreover we saw the children of Anak there.

31 But the men that went up with him said, **We be not able to go up against the people; for they are stronger than we.**

32 And **they brought up an evil report of the land** which they had searched unto the children of Israel, saying, The land, through which we have gone to search it, is a land that eateth up the inhabitants thereof; and all the people that we saw in it are men of a great stature.

33 And **there we saw the giants,** the sons of Anak, which come of the giants: and we were in our own sight as grasshoppers, and so we were in their sight. (Numbers 13)

Despite all the miracles God performed in Egypt and afterward, those leaders still did not believe God could accomplish miracles "big" enough to remove the giants or penetrate their fortified cities.

14 **Is any thing too hard for the Lord**? (Genesis 18)

26 Then came the word of the Lord unto Jeremiah, saying,
27 Behold, I am the Lord, the God of all flesh: **is there any thing too hard for me**? (Jeremiah 32)

37 For with **God nothing shall be impossible.** (Luke 1)

Instead of *faith*, they manifested *fear* and spread that fear. They were responsible not only for their unbelief but for the unbelief of others. God did not take kindly to the misuse of their influence.

## Unfaithful & Disobedient

We'll need faith stronger than the disobedient Israelites if we will enter our Lands of Promise.

> 11 Surely none of the men that came up out of Egypt, from twenty years old and upward, shall see the land which I sware unto Abraham, unto Isaac, and unto Jacob; **because they have not wholly followed me** (Numbers 32)
>
> 6 But **without faith it is impossible to please him:** for he that cometh to God must believe that he is, and that he is a rewarder of them that diligently seek him. (Hebrews 11)

## Unrighteous

The example of Abraham and his faithfulness was known to the children of Israel. From Abraham's account, we see that God views *faithfulness* as a form of *righteousness*.

> 18 Who against hope believed in hope, that he might become the father of many nations, according to that which was spoken, So shall thy seed be.
> 19 **And being not weak in faith,** he considered not his own body now dead, when he was about an hundred years old, neither yet the

deadness of Sara's womb:
20 **He staggered not at the promise of God through unbelief;** but was strong in faith, giving glory to God;
21 And being **fully persuaded that, what he had promised, he was able also to perform.**
22 And **THEREFORE IT WAS IMPUTED TO HIM FOR RIGHTEOUSNESS.** (Romans 4)

*Righteousness* can be considered another *prerequisite* for entering your Lands of Promise. We learn from this that whatever Our Lord commands, we should do it faithfully.

## SOME DID ENTER

A lesser-known fact in the account of the children of Israel is that some of them were permitted to enter their Lands of Promise *immediately*, namely Joshua and Caleb and their families.

### Why They Entered

Unlike the unfaithful elders who returned with an evil report and turned the people against God, Joshua and Caleb did the opposite. They encouraged the people *not* to go against God.

> 9 Only **rebel not ye against the Lord** (Numbers 14)

The children of Israel responded with anger and wanted to kill Joshua and Caleb.

> 10 But **all the congregation bade stone them with stones.** (Numbers 14)

Fortunately, Our Lord intervened and saved them from certain death. And luckily for the children of Israel, Moses spoke to Our Lord on their behalf and saved them from sure destruction.

> 10 **And the glory of the Lord appeared** in the tabernacle of the congregation before all the children of Israel.
> 15 Now **if thou shalt kill all this people as one man,** then the nations which have heard the fame of thee will speak, saying,
> 16 Because the Lord was not able to bring this people into the land which he sware unto them, therefore he hath slain them in the wilderness. (Numbers 14)

So Joshua, Caleb, and their families were allowed to enter the Lands of Promise immediately. Note my points in the following stanza.

> 24 But my servant Caleb, because **he had ANOTHER SPIRIT with him (1)**, and **hath FOLLOWED ME FULLY (2)**, him will I bring into the land whereinto he went; and **his seed shall POSSESS IT**.
> 30 Doubtless ye shall not come into the land, concerning which I sware to make you dwell therein, **save Caleb the son of Jephunneh, and**

**Joshua the son of Nun.**
38 But **Joshua** the son of Nun, and **Caleb** the son of Jephunneh, which were of the men that went to search the land, **LIVED STILL.** (Numbers 14)

12 Save **Caleb** the son of Jephunneh the Kenezite, and **Joshua** the son of Nun: for **they have WHOLLY FOLLOWED the Lord (2).**
13 And the Lord's anger was kindled against Israel, and he **made them wander in the wilderness forty years**, until all the generation, that had done evil in the sight of the Lord, was consumed. (Numbers 32)

36 Save **Caleb** the son of Jephunneh; he shall see it, and to him will I give the land that he hath trodden upon, **and to his children, because he hath WHOLLY FOLLOWED the Lord (2).**
37 Also the **Lord was angry with me for your sakes**, saying, **Thou also shalt not go in thither.**
38 But **Joshua** the son of Nun, which standeth before thee, he shall go in thither: encourage him: for he shall cause Israel to inherit it.
39 Moreover your little ones, which ye said should be a prey, **and your children, which in that day had no knowledge between good and evil, they SHALL GO IN THITHER,** and unto them will I give it, and they shall possess it. (Deuteronomy 1)

## POINTS

These points enabled Joshua, Caleb, and their families to enter their Lands of Promise.

**1. Had Another Spirit**

An element overlooked in the account of the children of Israel is *spiritual warfare*, which has not been portrayed or represented as part of the drama. Yet, if Pharaoh's magicians could replicate some of Moses' miracles, it would be evidence that a very sophisticated evil was at work among them.

The following commandment is further proof of the presence of evil and deceiving spirits.

> 31 **Regard not them that have FAMILIAR SPIRITS,** neither seek after wizards, to be defiled by them: I am the Lord your God. (Leviticus 19)

> 6 **And the soul that turneth after such as have FAMILIAR SPIRITS,** and after wizards, to go a whoring after them, I will even set my face against that soul, and **will cut him off from among his people.** (Leviticus 20)

The Lord's statement about Caleb and Joshua being faithful and having "another spirit" in them is like saying, "Those other elders who were unfaithful had an *evil spirit* in them." From this, we learn that evil spirits and spiritual warfare were problematic for them and are not just modern phenomena. We must overcome this if we are going to enter our Lands of Promise.

## 2. Followed Fully

The need to carefully follow the commands of God cannot be overstated. The account of Moses and the children of Israel is replete with examples of over and under-obedience. Take the examples of Moses and Aaron. God *prevented* them from entering their Lands of Promise for doing *more* than instructed; i.e., they struck a rock to bring forth water instead of just commanding it.

> 7 And the Lord spake unto Moses, saying,
> 8 Take the rod, and gather thou the assembly together, thou, and Aaron thy brother, and **SPEAK ye unto the rock** before their eyes; and **it shall give forth his water**, and thou shalt bring forth to them water out of the rock: so thou shalt give the congregation and their beasts drink.
> 9 And Moses took the rod from before the Lord, as he commanded him.
> 10 And Moses and Aaron gathered the congregation together before the rock, and he said unto them, Hear now, ye rebels; must we fetch you water out of this rock?
> 11 And Moses lifted up his hand, and **with his rod he SMOTE THE ROCK TWICE**: and the water came out abundantly, and the congregation drank, and their beasts also.
> 12 And the Lord spake unto Moses and Aaron,

Because ye believed me not, to sanctify me in the eyes of the children of Israel, therefore ye shall not bring this congregation into the land which I have given them. (Numbers 20)

24 **Aaron** shall be gathered unto his people: for **he shall not enter into the land** which I have given unto the children of Israel, **because ye REBELLED AGAINST MY WORD at the water of Meribah.** (Numbers 20)

12 And the Lord said unto **Moses**, Get thee up into this mount Abarim, and see the land which I have given unto the children of Israel. 13 And when thou hast seen it, thou also shalt be gathered unto thy people, as Aaron thy brother was gathered.
14 For **ye REBELLED AGAINST MY COMMANDMENT** in the desert of Zin, in the strife of the congregation, to sanctify me at the water before their eyes: that is **the water of Meribah** in Kadesh in the wilderness of Zin. (Numbers 27)

The name of the water has relevance. The Hebrew word *Meribah* identifies the *location,* and the Hebrew word *Marah* identifies the *disobedience.*

24 Aaron shall be gathered unto his people: for he shall not enter into the land which I have given unto the children of Israel, **because ye rebelled against my word at the water of Meribah.** (Numbers 20)

# WATERS OF MERIBAH

There are three *Types* associated with the account of the *Waters of Meribah*.

## Rock

It's interesting to note that once again, water was brought out of a *rock*, like at Horeb, but it could have just as easily come forth out of the ground. God's use of a *rock* has meaning and is a *Type* of *Christ*.

> 4 And did all drink the same spiritual drink: for they drank of that **spiritual Rock** that followed them: and that **Rock was Christ**. (1 Corinthians 10)

Many scriptures associate "rock" and "stone" with Our Lord.

> 24 But his bow abode in strength, and the arms of his hands were made strong by the hands of the mighty God of Jacob; from thence is the shepherd, the **STONE of Israel** (Genesis 49)

> 4 **He is the ROCK,** his work is perfect: for all his ways are judgment: a God of truth and without iniquity, just and right is he. (Deuteronomy 32)

> 15 But Jeshurun waxed fat, and kicked: thou

art waxen fat, thou art grown thick, thou art covered with fatness; then he forsook God which made him, and lightly esteemed the **ROCK OF HIS SALVATION**. (Deuteronomy 32)

2 There is none holy as the Lord: for there is none beside thee: **neither is there ANY ROCK like our God**. (1 Samuel 2)

2 And he said, **The Lord is MY ROCK,** and my fortress, and my deliverer;
3 **The God of MY ROCK**; in him will I trust: he is my shield, and the horn of my salvation, my high tower, and my refuge, my saviour; thou savest me from violence. (2 Samuel 22)

2 The Spirit of the Lord spake by me, and his word was in my tongue.
3 The God of Israel said, **the ROCK OF ISRAEL spake to me**, He that ruleth over men must be just, ruling in the fear of God. (2 Samuel 23:2–3)

2 **The Lord is MY ROCK**, and my fortress, and my deliverer; my God, my strength, in whom I will trust; my buckler, and the horn of my salvation, and my high tower. (Psalms 18)

31 For who is God save the Lord? or who is a **ROCK save our God**? (Psalms 18)

46 The Lord liveth; and **blessed be MY ROCK**; and let the God of my salvation be exalted. (Psalms 18)

2 From the end of the Earth will I cry unto thee, when my heart is overwhelmed: lead me to **THE ROCK that is higher than I**. (Psalms 61)

2 He only is **MY ROCK and my salvation**; he is my defence; I shall not be greatly moved.
6 He only is **MY ROCK and my salvation**: he is my defence; I shall not be moved.
7 In God is my salvation and my glory: **THE ROCK of my strength and my refuge**, is in God. (Psalms 62)

22 **THE STONE** which the **builders refused** is become the **head STONE of the CORNER**. (Psalms 118)

42 Jesus saith unto them, Did ye never read in the scriptures, **THE STONE which the builders rejected**, the same is become the **head of the CORNER** (Matthew 21)

14 And he shall be for a sanctuary; but for a **STONE OF STUMBLING and for a ROCK OF OFFENCE** to both the houses of Israel, for a gin and for a snare to the inhabitants of Jerusalem. (Isaiah 8)

1 Hearken to me, ye that follow after righteousness, ye that seek the Lord: look unto the **ROCK whence ye are hewn**, and to the hole of the pit whence ye are digged. (Isaiah 51)

11 **This is THE STONE** which was set at nought

of you builders, which is become the head of the corner. (Acts 4)

33 As it is written, Behold, **I lay in Sion a STUMBLINGSTONE and ROCK OF OFFENCE**: and whosoever believeth on him shall not be ashamed. (Romans 9)

8 And a **STONE OF STUMBLING, and a ROCK OF OFFENCE**, even to them which stumble at the word, being disobedient: whereunto also they were appointed. (1 Peter 2)

Thus, God's repeated use of "rock" is a *Type* of Christ.

## Water

*Water* is the next *Type*, which flows out of the rock (Christ). What it represents must have something to do with Our Lord, and it does.

10 Jesus answered and said unto her, If thou knewest the gift of God, and who it is that saith to thee, Give me to drink; thou wouldest have asked of him, and **HE would have given thee LIVING WATER.**
11 The woman saith unto him, Sir, thou hast nothing to draw with, and the well is deep: from whence then hast thou that living water?
12 Art thou greater than our father Jacob, which gave us the well, and drank thereof himself, and his children, and his cattle?
13 Jesus answered and said unto her, Whoso-

ever drinketh of this water shall thirst again:
14 But **whosoever drinketh of THE WATER that I SHALL GIVE him shall NEVER THIRST; but MY ROCK that I SHALL GIVE him shall be in him a well of WATER springing up into EVERLASTING LIFE.**
15 The woman saith unto him, Sir, give me this water, that I thirst not, neither come hither to draw. (John 4)

Water is essential for life. Our Lord is saying He is to our soul what water is to the flesh, and we cannot inherit Everlasting Life without Him. The key to harnessing this "soul water" is to believe in Our Lord.

> 35 He that **BELIEVETH** on me shall **never thirst**. (John 6)

> 37 In the last day, that great day of the feast, Jesus stood and cried, saying, **If any man THIRST, let him come unto me, and DRINK.** 38 **He that BELIEVETH on me**, as the scripture hath said, **OUT OF HIS BELLY SHALL FLOW RIVERS OF LIVING WATER.** (John 7)

This concept of Our Lord being "living water" appears to be a genuine dynamic because He is both the *Creator* and *Sustainer* of life.

> 1 In the beginning was the Word, and the Word was with God, and the Word was God.
> 2 The same was in the beginning with God.
> 3 **All things were MADE by HIM;** and without

him was not any thing made that was made.
4 **In HIM was LIFE;** and the life was the light of men.
10 He was in the world, and the world was made by him, and the world knew him not.
12 But as many as **RECEIVED HIM,** to them gave he **power to become the sons of God**, even to **them that BELIEVE on HIS NAME**: (John 1)

12 Then spake Jesus again unto them, saying, I am the light of the world: **he that FOLLOWETH ME** shall not walk in darkness, but **shall have the LIGHT of LIFE.** (John 8)

11 And this is the record, that God hath given to us eternal life, and this **LIFE IS IN HIS SON.** 12 **He that HATH THE SON hath LIFE;** and he that hath not the Son of God hath not life. (1 John 5)

Thus, both accounts of water gushing from a rock were *Types* of Our Lord and His saving grace.

## Misuse

The third *Type* represents a common practice today of misusing God's anointing, Jesus' name, or His power. It's hard to imagine anyone exploiting such things, but Our Lord warned that it would happen, and it's what kept Aaron and Moses out of their Lands of Promise:

21 Not every one that saith unto me, Lord, Lord, shall enter into the kingdom of Heaven; but he that doeth the will of my Father which is in Heaven.
22 Many will say to me in that day, **Lord, Lord, have we not prophesied in thy name? and in thy name have cast out devils? and in thy name done many wonderful works**?
23 And then will I profess unto them, **I never knew you: depart from me**, ye that work iniquity. (Matthew 7)

1 Though I speak with the tongues of men and of angels, and have not charity, I am become as sounding brass, or a tinkling cymbal.
2 And **though I have the gift of prophecy**, and **understand all mysteries**, and **all knowledge**; and though I **have all faith**, so that I could remove mountains, and have not charity, **I am nothing**.
3 And though I bestow all my goods to feed the poor, and though I give my body to be burned, and have not charity, **it profiteth me nothing**. (1 Corinthians 13)

We must not do more than He said. The account of Saul *not* destroying everything as instructed by God is one example.

3 Now go [Saul] and smite Amalek, and utterly **destroy all that they have, and spare them not**; but slay both man and woman, infant and suckling, ox and sheep, camel and ass.
9 But Saul and the people spared Agag, and

the best of the sheep, and of the oxen, and of the fatlings, and the lambs, and all that was good, and **would not utterly destroy them**: but every thing that was vile and refuse, that they destroyed utterly.
10 Then came the word of the Lord unto Samuel, saying,
11 **It repenteth me that I have set up Saul to be king**: for he is turned back from following me, and **hath not performed my commandments**. And it grieved Samuel; and he cried unto the Lord all night. (1 Samuel 15)

22 Behold, **TO OBEY IS BETTER** than sacrifice, **and to hearken** than the fat of rams. (1 Samuel 15)

Even zealousness can be a sin.

2 For I bear them record that they have a **ZEAL OF GOD**, but not according to knowledge.
3 For they being ignorant of God's righteousness, and **going about to establish their OWN RIGHTEOUSNESS,** have not submitted themselves unto the righteousness of God. (Romans 10)

A pronounced example of this today is "Churchianity." As each church "establishes its own righteousness," they divide our communities. The division is a *cardinal sin*. Cardinal sins are based on *Proverbs* 6, which says:

16 These six things doth the Lord hate: yea,

seven are an abomination unto him:
17 A **proud look**, a lying tongue, and hands that shed innocent blood,
18 An heart that deviseth wicked imaginations, feet that be swift in running to mischief,
19 A false witness that speaketh lies, **and he that SOWETH DISCORD among brethren**. (Proverbs 6)

Churches are largely unaware of this, but Our Lord wants unity, first and foremost.

> 21 **THAT THEY ALL MAY BE ONE;** as thou, Father, art in me, and I in thee, that they also may be one in us: **THAT THE WORLD MAY BELIEVE** that thou hast sent me.(John 17)

Let's not forget all of our *works* are as filthy rags.

> 5 **Thou meetest him that rejoiceth and worketh righteousness,** those that remember thee in thy ways: behold, thou art wroth; for we have sinned: in those is continuance, and we shall be saved.
> 6 But we are all as an unclean thing, and **all our righteousnesses are as filthy rags;** and we all do fade as a leaf; and our iniquities, like the wind, have taken us away. (Isaiah 64)

God prefers obedience because His ways are higher than ours, and our minds cannot decipher *all* the purposes of God.

> 8 For **my thoughts are not your thoughts,**

neither are your ways my ways, saith the Lord. 9 For as the Heavens are higher than the Earth, **so are my ways higher than your ways, and my thoughts than your thoughts.** (Isaiah 55)

We should think about our choices and actions, for the ramifications of our choices extend far beyond ourselves to our children and their children.

5 Thou shalt not bow down thyself to them, nor serve them: for I the Lord thy God am a jealous God, **visiting the iniquity of the fathers upon the children unto the third and fourth generation of them that hate me;** (Exodus 20)

7 Keeping mercy for thousands, forgiving iniquity and transgression and sin, and that will by no means clear the guilty; **visiting the iniquity of the fathers upon the children, and upon the children's children, unto the third and to the fourth generation.** (Exodus 34)

18 The Lord is longsuffering, and of great mercy, forgiving iniquity and transgression, and by no means clearing the guilty, **visiting the iniquity of the fathers upon the children unto the third and fourth generation.** (Numbers 14)

5 Then I will set my face against that man, **and against his family,** and will cut him off, and all that go a whoring after him, to commit whore-

dom with Molech, from among their people. (Leviticus 20)

Children are innocent before God, as He said.

> 39 your **children,** which in that day **had no knowledge between good and evil** (Deuteronomy 1)

However, the consequences of parents' actions *can* affect the children; that's God's law. As we have already seen, the children of the wicked elders had to wander for forty years because of their parents' actions; remember that children learn by example. Conversely, the children of faithful elders could enter their lands right away.

## PROVOCATION

Paul recognized that the account of Moses and the children of Israel was a *Type* and *Shadow* to prepare us for entering into God's rest in our Lands of Promise. Paul confirms many of the same points in the following stanza and refers to the whole affair as their "Provocation" (note Paul's emphasis on *hardened hearts* and *unbelief*).

> 7 Wherefore as the Holy Ghost saith, To day if ye will hear his voice,
> 8 **Harden not your hearts, as in THE PROVOCATION,** in the day of temptation in the wilderness:

9 When your fathers **tempted me,** proved me, and saw my works forty years.

10 Wherefore I was grieved with that generation, and said, They do alway err in their heart; and they have not known my ways.

11 So I sware in my wrath, They shall **not enter into my rest.**

12 Take heed, brethren, lest there be in any of you an **evil heart of unbelief, in departing from the living God.**

13 But exhort one another daily, while it is called To day; lest any of you be **hardened through the deceitfulness of sin.**

14 For we are made partakers of Christ, if we **hold the beginning of our confidence steadfast unto the end;**

15 While it is said, To day if ye will **hear his voice, harden not your hearts, as in the PROVOCATION.**

16 For some, when they had heard, did provoke: **howbeit not all** that came out of Egypt by Moses.

17 But with whom was he grieved forty years? **was it not with them that had sinned,** whose carcases fell in the wilderness?

18 And to whom sware he that they should not enter into his rest, but to **them that believed not**?

19 So we see that **they could not enter in because of unbelief.** (Hebrews 3)

# OUR LANDS OF PROMISE

The children of Israel had to travel out to meet God before entering their Lands of Promise. We, too, must travel out to meet God before entering our Lands of Promise. They *formally* met God at Mt. Sinai. This *Type* foreshadows our journeying out to meet God in *The Rapture*.

Where will the raptured go? Not straight to God's throne, but into the New Jerusalem. The New Jerusalem will be our Mt. Sinai, and we will meet Our Lord there. He will meet us "halfway" as He did with the children of Israel. The prophesied New Jerusalem will come from the Third Heaven and retrieve the Raptured.

## New Jerusalem

John describes the *New Jerusalem* as a "city."

> 12 The name of the **CITY of my God**, which is new Jerusalem (Revelation 3)

> 2 And I John saw the **HOLY CITY**, **new Jerusalem** (Revelation 21)

> 10 shewed me that **GREAT CITY**, the **holy Jerusalem** (Revelation 21)

> 14 may enter in through the gates into the **CITY** (Revelation 22)

> 19 out of the **HOLY CITY** (Revelation 22)

**How Large Is It?**

The size of *The New Jerusalem* is known. According to John, it's *1500 miles wide by 1500 miles long by 1500 miles high.*

> 9 And there came unto me one of the seven angels which had the seven vials full of the seven last plagues, and talked with me, saying, Come hither, I will shew thee the bride, the Lamb's wife.
> 10 And he carried me away in the spirit to a great and high mountain, and shewed me that **GREAT CITY, the holy Jerusalem,** descending out of Heaven from God,
> 11 Having the glory of God: and her light was like unto a stone most precious, even like a jasper stone, clear as crystal;
> 12 And had a wall great and high, and had twelve gates, and at the gates twelve angels, and names written thereon, which are the names of the twelve tribes of the children of Israel:
> 13 On the east three gates; on the north three gates; on the south three gates; and on the west three gates.
> 14 And the wall of the city had twelve foundations, and in them the names of the twelve apostles of the Lamb.
> 15 And he that talked with me had a golden reed to measure the city, and the gates thereof, and the wall thereof.
> 16 And the city **lieth FOURSQUARE, and the**

**length is as large as the breadth: and he measured the CITY with the reed, twelve thousand furlongs. The length and the breadth and the height of it are equal.**

17 And he measured the wall thereof, an hundred and forty and four cubits, according to the measure of a man, that is, of the angel.

18 And the building of the wall of it was of jasper: and the city was pure gold, like unto clear glass.

19 And the foundations of the wall of the city were garnished with all manner of precious stones. The first foundation was jasper; the second, sapphire; the third, a chalcedony; the fourth, an emerald;

20 The fifth, sardonyx; the sixth, sardius; the seventh, chrysolite; the eighth, beryl; the ninth, a topaz; the tenth, a chrysoprasus; the eleventh, a jacinth; the twelfth, an amethyst.

21 And the twelve gates were twelve pearls; every several gate was of one pearl: and the street of the city was pure gold, as it were transparent glass.

22 And I saw no temple therein: for the Lord God Almighty and the Lamb are the temple of it.

23 And **the CITY** had no need of the sun, neither of the moon, to shine in it: for the glory of God did lighten it, and the Lamb is the light thereof.

24 And **the nations of them which are saved shall walk in the light of it**: and the **kings of the Earth do bring their glory and honour**

**into it**.
25 And the gates of it shall not be shut at all by day: for there shall be no night there.
26 And **they shall bring the glory and honour of the nations into it**.
27 And **there shall in no wise enter into it any thing that defileth**, neither whatsoever worketh abomination, or maketh a lie: but **they which are written in the Lamb's book of life**. (Revelation 21)

## Where Is It?

The location of *The New Jerusalem* is also known. It currently resides before the throne of God and will move from there to a point above the Earth. This event will create *The Sign* of Jesus' Coming.

> 30 And **then shall appear THE SIGN of the Son of man in Heaven** (Matthew 24)

God does use signs to give people a *witness* and a *warning*.

> 4 **God also bearing them WITNESS, both with SIGNS** and wonders, and with divers miracles, and gifts of the Holy Ghost, according to his own will. (Hebrews 2)

There are several mentions of The New Jerusalem *coming down*. It will come down *partway* and then fully at the end of The Millennium.

> 12 The name of the **city of my God,** which is

**new Jerusalem,** which **cometh down** out of Heaven from my God (Revelation 3)

1 And I saw a new Heaven and a new Earth: for the first Heaven and the first Earth were passed away; and there was no more sea.
2 And I John saw the **holy city, new Jerusalem, coming down** from God out of Heaven, prepared as a bride adorned for her husband. (Revelation 21)

**Who May Enter It?**

The requirement to enter *The New Jerusalem* will be the same requirement that the children of Israel had for entering their Lands of Promise: obedience.

> 35 Surely there shall **not one of these men of this evil generation see that good land,** which I sware to give unto your fathers,
> 36 **Save Caleb** the son of Jephunneh; **he shall see it, and to him will I give the land** that he hath trodden upon, and to his children, because **he hath wholly followed the Lord.** (Deuteronomy 1)
>
> 14 **BLESSED ARE THEY THAT DO HIS COMMANDMENTS,** that they may have right to the tree of life, and **may enter in through the gates into the city.** (Revelation 22)

## Who Has Seen It?

Are there any modern-day "scouts" who have seen *The New Jerusalem* and returned to tell about it? Yes.

- **Percy Collett (1902-1998)** in *I Walked in Heaven With Jesus*, 1984; *Percy Collett's Map of Heaven*, 2022,[1] and 35 hours of recordings.[2]
- **Oden Hetrick (1922-2001)** in *Inside the Gates of Heaven*[3] plus a taped interview called *The Testimony of Heaven – Inside the Holy City of God*.[4]
- **Richard Sigmund (1941-2010)** in *My Time In Heaven* – 2009

After the festivities of the Wedding Banquet, some attendees will stay in the Third Heaven where God resides, but others will return to Earth to reign with Our Lord for a thousand years.

Notes

1. https://lionandlamb.net/books/percy-colletts-map-of-heaven/.
2. https://web.archive.org/web/20160125131914/http://beholy.be/percy.htm.
3. https://odenhetrick.com/read.html.
4. https://www.youtube.com/watch?v=S1QJ6rK5CMQ.

# SIGNS & WONDERS

One of the things that Moses did by the power of God was to show forth many "signs and wonders." Moses coined that phrase, which many ministers have since used. According to Moses, God "hardened" Pharaoh's heart repeatedly so He could manifest more and more *signs* and *wonders*.

> 1 And the Lord said unto Moses, See, I have made thee a god to Pharaoh: and Aaron thy brother shall be thy prophet.
> 2 Thou shalt speak all that I command thee: and Aaron thy brother shall speak unto Pharaoh, that he send the children of Israel out of his land.
> 3 And **I will harden Pharaoh's heart**, and **multiply my signs and my wonders** in the land of Egypt. (Exodus 7)

One of the reasons God did this was so His name would be known throughout the Earth for all time.

> 16 And in very deed for this cause have I raised thee up, for to shew in thee my power; and **that MY NAME may be DECLARED throughout ALL THE EARTH**. (Exodus 9)

Another reason was so the people would revere Him with a righteous fear.

> 31 And Israel **saw that GREAT WORK** which

the Lord did upon the Egyptians: and **the people FEARED the Lord**, and believed the Lord, and his servant Moses. (Exodus 14)

And to deter the people from sinning.

> 18 And all the people saw the thunderings, and the lightnings, and the noise of the trumpet, and the mountain smoking: and when the people saw it, they removed, and stood afar off.
> 19 And they said unto Moses, Speak thou with us, and we will hear: but let not God speak with us, lest we die.
> 20 And Moses said unto the people, Fear not: for God is come to prove you, and **that his FEAR may be before your faces, THAT YE SIN NOT**. (Exodus 20)

Do people fear God today? Even among Believers, there seems to be a lack of Godly fear. God's compelling act *was* The Exodus, which has been devalued by scientists and theologians who question the narrative. Others do not believe there is any evidence at all. For those reasons, I include the following.

## EXODUS EVIDENCES

Where would you go as a Christian to make a pilgrimage? Probably Jerusalem. Where would you go as a Jew to make a pilgrimage? Jerusalem also.

Even the general public is fond of making pilgrimages to Jerusalem.

> **Pilgrimage:** a journey, especially a long one, made to some sacred place as an act of religious devotion. –*Random House Dictionary*

Jerusalem seems to be one of the most sacred places on Earth, yet God did not descend there; He descended on Mt. Sinai in Arabia. Where did the apostle Paul go to make his pilgrimage after becoming a Christian? To the Mt. Sinai in *Arabia,* not the one inaccurately named in the Sinai Peninsula.

> 15 But when it pleased God, who separated me from my mother's womb, and called me by his grace,
> 16 To reveal his Son in me, that I might preach him among the heathen; immediately I conferred not with flesh and blood:
> 17 **Neither went I up to Jerusalem** to them which were apostles before me; **but I went into ARABIA,** and returned again unto Damascus. (Galatians 1)

If a person wanted to go to the most sacred place on Earth, as Paul did, they would go to Mt. Sinai in Arabia. So why haven't Jews, Christians, or the public taken pilgrimages there? From what I can gather, there are two reasons. First, most people think it's in the Sinai Peninsula. Second, it was made inaccessible by the Saudi government.

Now that researchers have looked in (Midian) Arabia, where the scriptures say to look, the evidence they found there is significant.

## Dr. Frank Moore Cross

Dr. Frank Moore Cross, retired Professor of Hebrew at Harvard University, concluded that Sinai was in Midian Arabia, not the Sinai Peninsula.

> One of the most vexing problems in biblical archaeology is establishing the route taken by the Israelites when they left Egypt. Many theories have been proposed for tracking the Exodus – a northern route along the Mediterranean called the "Way of the Land of the Philistines" or the "Way of the Sea," a central route called the "Way of Shur" and a southern route that passes by Jebel Musa, the mountain traditionally identified as Mount Sinai. **Frank Moore Cross considers efforts to locate Mount Sinai in the Sinai Peninsula misguided**. He believes the Israelites wandered through the **land of Midian**, east of the Gulf of Eilat (modern northwest Saudi Arabia).[1]

The place where the Israelites dwelt had to sustain a large group of people, which the Sinai Peninsula could not do. There was also the known element of Moses marrying a Midianite and living in Midian for *forty years*. The Jewish historian *Josephus* wrote that Mt. Sinai was the tallest mountain in Midian,[2] which Professor Cross identified as *Jebel el-Lawz*.

## Dr. Glen A. Fritz

A second example is Dr. Glen A. Fritz. He was born in 1949, graduated from dental school in 1973, served as a captain in the Air Force after college, and practiced as an oral surgeon for fourteen years in Vero Beach, Florida. In 1996, he visited Israel and was profoundly affected. He began to study Hebrew and traveled throughout Egypt, Israel, and Jordan.

*The Lost Sea of the Exodus:* A *Modern Geographical Analysis*, ©Glen A. Fritz

To facilitate his ability to solve the *Exodus* question, he enrolled in Texas State University and completed a PhD in *Environmental Geography*. His doctoral thesis was *The Lost Sea of the Exodus: A Modern Geographical Analysis*.

In his doctoral thesis, Fritz came to the following conclusion.

**Yam Suph**, the **Hebrew name** for the **Sea of the Exodus**, has probably been called the 'Red

Sea' or the 'Sea of Reeds' and has been assigned locations in the proximity of Egypt. However, such locations do not harmonize with the geography of *Yam Suph* given in the Hebrew Scriptures. The confusion began over 2000 years ago, when the Septuagint Bible equated *Yam Suph* with the deficient Greek concept of the Red Sea.

Although this 'Red Sea' tradition for the Exodus has largely been discarded, it has been replaced with problematic 'Reed Sea' theories that have linked *Yam Suph* with various inland Egyptian estuaries. **This research demonstrates that the biblical identity of *Yam Suph* corresponds solely with the modern Gulf of Aqaba** and reveals how this understanding was lost in antiquity.[3]

## Dr. David Kim

©Ross Patterson, *youtube.com/watch?v=RxY7-x6V3Vs*

A third example is Dr. David Kim of Seoul, Korea,

who was the personal physician of a Saudi prince for sixteen years. During that time, he made many trips to the Midian area and documented what he saw. The following pictures are from his PowerPoint presentation.[4]

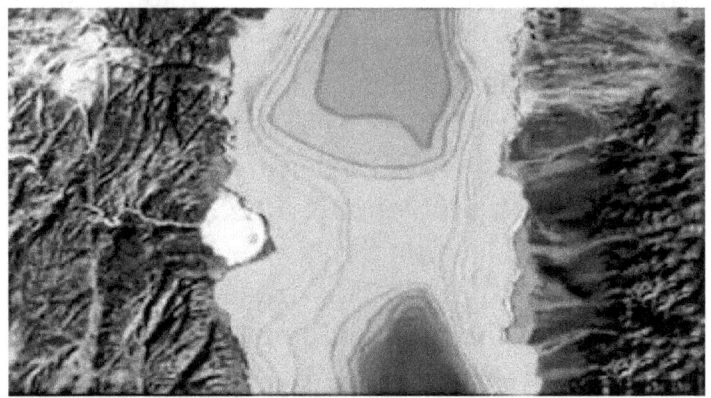

East Branch of the Red Sea, Called Gulf of Aqaba

As seen in the above picture, there's an underwater "highway" in the east branch of the *Red Sea* known as the *Gulf of Aqaba*, where Moses and the children of Israel crossed.

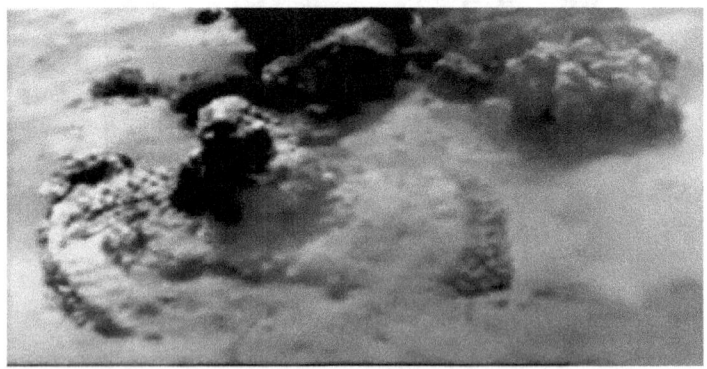

Chariot Wheel Covered With Coral

Many unusual clumps of coral along that underwater stretch of highway resemble chariot debris and chariot wheels. Those who have seen the area say it looks like a bomb went off.

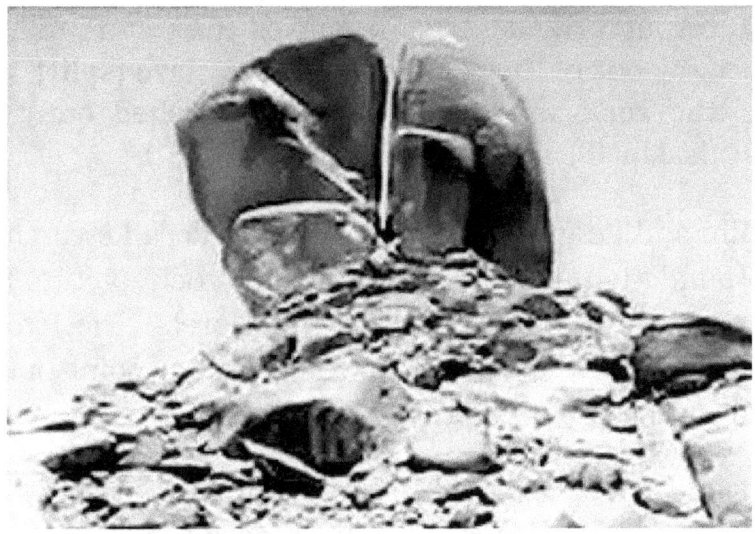

*Split Rock of Horeb*

Equally astonishing is the rock that God split when Moses struck it with his staff, and water gushed forth like "rivers."

> 6 Behold, I will stand before thee there upon the rock in Horeb; and thou shalt **smite the rock**, and there shall come water out of it, that the people may drink. And Moses did so in the sight of the elders of Israel. (Exodus 17)

> 15 He **clave [split] the rocks** in the wilderness, and gave them drink as out of the great

depths.
16 He brought streams also out of the rock, and **caused waters to run down like rivers**. (Psalms 78)

21 And they thirsted not when he led them through the deserts: he caused the waters to flow out of the rock for them: **he clave [split] the rock** also, and the **waters gushed out**. (Isaiah 48)

Jim and Penny Caldwell of the *Split Rock Research Foundation* discovered the split rock pictured above. They named it "Rock of Horeb." The two items that the Caldwells would like to point out from the above verses are as follows:

**a.** He "clave the rocks" is a shadow of what will happen when Jesus steps down onto the *Mount of Olives*.

> 4 And **his feet shall stand in that day upon the mount of Olives**, which is before Jerusalem on the east, and **the mount of Olives shall cleave in the midst thereof** toward the east and toward the west, and there shall be a very great valley; and half of the mountain shall remove toward the north, and half of it toward the south. (Zechariah 14)

**b.** For the water to "run down like rivers," the rock would have to be elevated, which it is.

*Side View, Man in the Circle, 7 Story High Scale*

Dr. David Kim says the *Rock of Horeb* is "seven stories high."

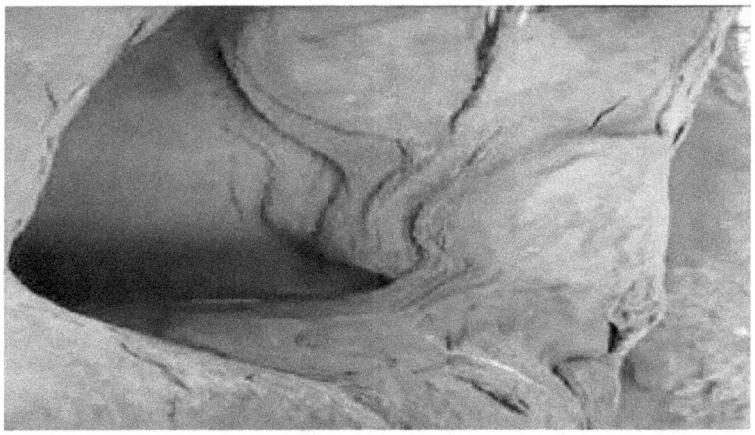

*Water Spout*

This photo shows a close-up of where the water gushed forth. The wear on the rocks and the direction of the wear is from water, yet it's in the middle of the desert.

Water Way

Remember that this area receives less than an inch of rain each year.

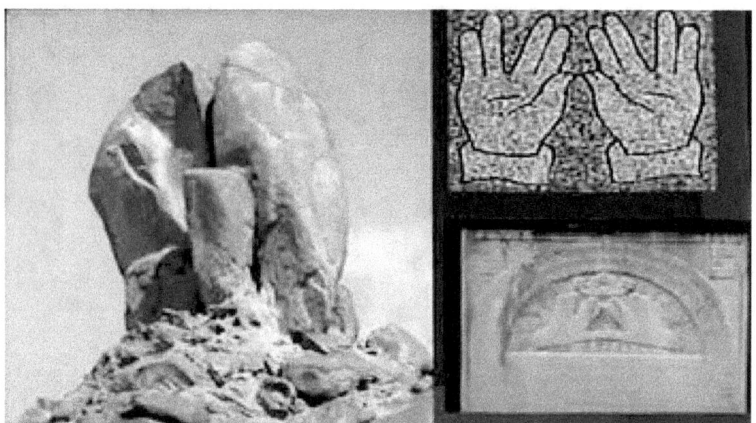

Aaronic Blessing

Dr. Kim believes the Jewish *Aaronic Blessing* hand sign symbolizes the miracle at the *Split Rock of Horeb*.

*Grinding Stone*

Grinding stones (for manna) are found throughout the area by the *thousands*.

> 23 And he said unto them, This is that which the Lord hath said, To morrow is the rest of the holy sabbath unto the Lord: **bake that which ye will bake to day**, and seethe that ye will seethe; and that which remaineth over lay up for you to be kept until the morning. (Exodus 16)

The following carvings depicting a loosed sandal are found all along the route the children of Israel went, and this is how they claimed the land.

*Land Claims*

**24 Every place whereon the soles of your feet shall tread shall be yours**: from the wilderness and Lebanon, from the river, the river Euphrates, even unto the uttermost sea shall your coast be. (Deuteronomy 11)

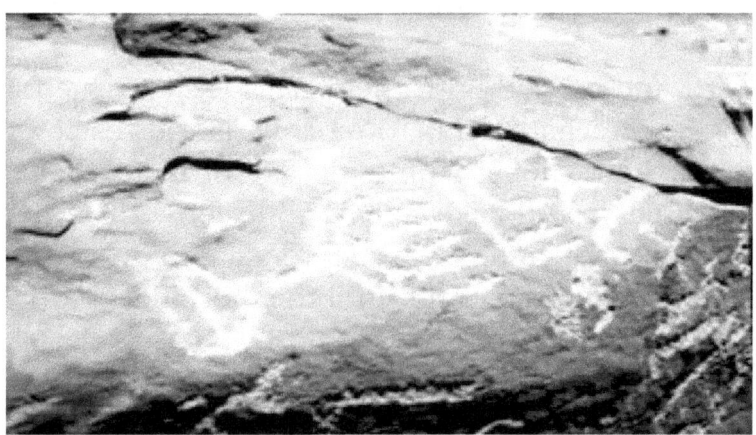

*Menorah*

Near the bottom of the true Mt. Sinai, Dr. Kim discovered the engraving of a menorah, pictured above, which he claims is the oldest known menorah.

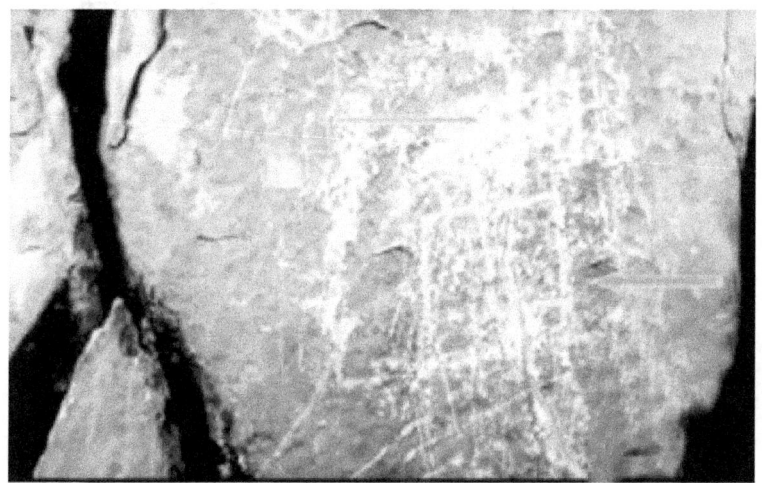

*Defaced Serpent on a Pole*

This photo shows the engraving of a serpent on a pole, as described in the Bible. According to Dr. Kim, Arab soldiers were instructed to deface it.

> 9 And Moses made a **serpent of brass, and put it upon a pole**, and it came to pass, that if a serpent had bitten any man, when he beheld the serpent of brass, he lived. (Numbers 21)

Pictured below is a cedar tree trunk measuring *eight feet in diameter*. It could be like the bush Moses saw "on fire" but was not consumed.

> 1 Now Moses kept the flock of Jethro his father in law, the priest of Midian: and he led the flock to the backside of the desert, and **came**

Signs & Wonders | 115

**to the mountain of God, even to Horeb.**
2 And the angel of the Lord appeared unto him in a flame of fire out of the midst of a bush: and he looked, and, behold, the **bush burned with fire, and the bush was not consumed.** (Exodus 3)

*Eight Foot Wide Cedar Tree Trunk*

Almond trees can also grow in the area, confirming the Biblical account of Aaron's rod.

> 8 And it came to pass, that on the morrow Moses went into the tabernacle of witness; and, behold, the **rod of Aaron** for the house of Levi was budded, and brought forth **buds, and bloomed blossoms, and yielded almonds.** (Numbers 17)

Here's a picture of the true Mt. Sinai. The peak and surrounding area are dark, almost black, with a blue tint believed to be caused by the tremendous heat from the large fire cloud when God rested upon it.

Mt. Sinai and Elijah's Cave – Pic 1

The circle on the front-facing mountain is the cave of Elijah.

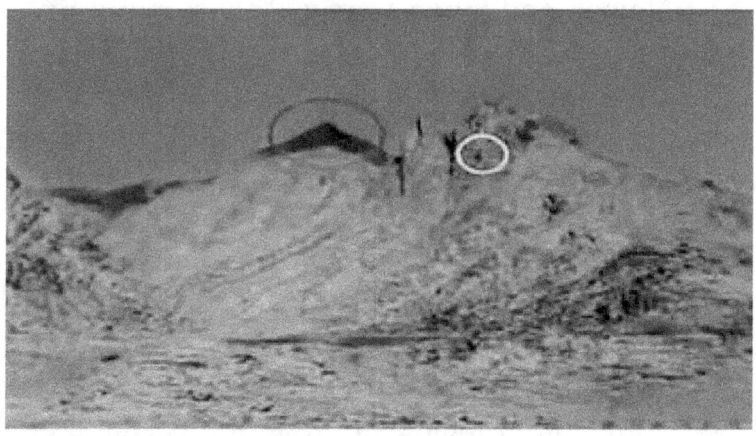

Mt. Sinai and Elijah's Cave – Pic 2

*View From Inside Elijah's Cave*

## Testimonies of Dr. Kim

The following testimonies by Dr. Kim are from his interview with Ross Patterson.[5]

@ 21:47 **It was like the cloud PILLAR. Then I followed** and when I arrived that **mountain was Jabel-Lawz.** And then I stopped there. When I got out of the car suddenly on my back was sunshine but **this BLACK CLOUD completely covered all around the mountain.** From inside started lightning, thunder, like when God appeared 3500 years before. I was afraid really. Yep, first trip. And suddenly **I fell down. I started to pray to God.** You know the **rain dropped** on my body and the **thunder,** the sound inside the mountain…Huge! It felt like an **earthquake shaking the ground.** I was afraid that some stones would fall down from the mountain, and **thunder** and **lightning**...After that I was afraid and prayed to God. "Please, we are sinful!"...Then I asked him [a bedouin], "Did you ever see something like this happen before?" He said that he's almost **80 years old**. He said, "**I've never seen this in all my life**. And this time is not the raining season.

### Jesus Appeared to Daughter

@ 32:51 Then she like this, "Papa, Papa. Jesus, Jesus." She is 10 years old. I say, "You dreamed." "No, no, no. This is the third time I have woken up now." I said, "How come?" "You know when I was sleeping, somebody called my name, 'Unson, Unson, Unson,' like this." And then she woke up, she found out, "**Something on the top of the mountain, a very strong light came to me. It said from the light, 'Unson, don't worry. I will take care of your family.'** "Then she was still sleepy. She slept. "And then again somebody called, 'Unson, Unson.' So now, the third time I woke up. **I am sure He is Jesus Christ.**"

### Plenty of Archaeological Evidence

@ 35:04 At that place [Arabia], **why are there JEWISH MARKS on it there**? And at that place, **why are there old HEBREW LETTERS there**? This is what I am saying, so we are still studying the **MENORAH inscriptions** with the **old letters**.

### Red Sea Crossing Pillar Hidden in the Sea Now

@ 39:53 He [a local boy] said almost **4m-5m under the sea, the stone pillar is there**. So if it really is King Solomon's Red Sea Crossing marker pillar, **Mt Sinai will move to Saudi Arabia**.

@ 40:53 I found out very strange pictures were there. As you know if you go to the Peru, Nazca area UNESCO are now controlling there. The biggest picture is 200m – 250m only. But here in the Midian wilderness stone structures, sometimes you can find 1.7km, sometimes you find 3km of the picture is there. But each one, there something meaningful. Something really strange, mysterious. But it took a huge amount of labour to build these structures. Who was there? Who had a big enough population to build them? Only the Hebrews.

### God Protected – 3500 Years

@ 46:13 If Mt Sinai was in an open place like Egypt or if Mt Sinai was in America or somewhere else, it would have been destroyed entirely, like Jerusalem. But this one, **for 3500 years, God protected it Himself!**

# Viveka Ponten

©Mary Nell Wyatt Lee, youtu.be/O5BeqMsWt8w

*Viveka Ponten* of Sweden traveled to Midian in 1997 and noticed that in the area in front of Elijah's cave is a large flat area where the children of Israel camped. Several large boulders seemed entirely out of place and were split in half. She recalled Elijah's encounter with God, and it was her opinion those boulders were the result of that meeting.[6]

> 7 And the angel of the Lord came again the second time, and touched him, and said, Arise and eat; because the journey is too great for thee.
> 8 And he arose, and did eat and drink, and went in the strength of that meat forty days and forty nights unto **HOREB the MOUNT of GOD**.
> 9 And he came thither **unto a CAVE, and lodged there**; and, behold, the word of the Lord came to him, and he said unto him, What doest thou here, Elijah?
> 10 And he said, I have been very jealous for the Lord God of hosts: for the children of Israel have forsaken thy covenant, thrown down

*Signs & Wonders*

thine altars, and slain thy prophets with the sword; and I, even **I only, am left**; and they seek my life, to take it away.

11 And he said, Go forth, and stand upon the mount before the Lord. And, behold, **the Lord passed by, and a great and strong wind rent the mountains, and brake in pieces the rocks** before the Lord; but the Lord was not in the wind: and after the wind an earthquake; but the Lord was not in the earthquake:

12 And after the earthquake a fire; but the Lord was not in the fire: and after the fire a still small voice.

13 And it was so, when Elijah heard it, that he wrapped his face in his mantle, and went out, and **stood in the entering in of the cave**. And, behold, there came a voice unto him, and said, What doest thou here, Elijah? (1 Kings 19)

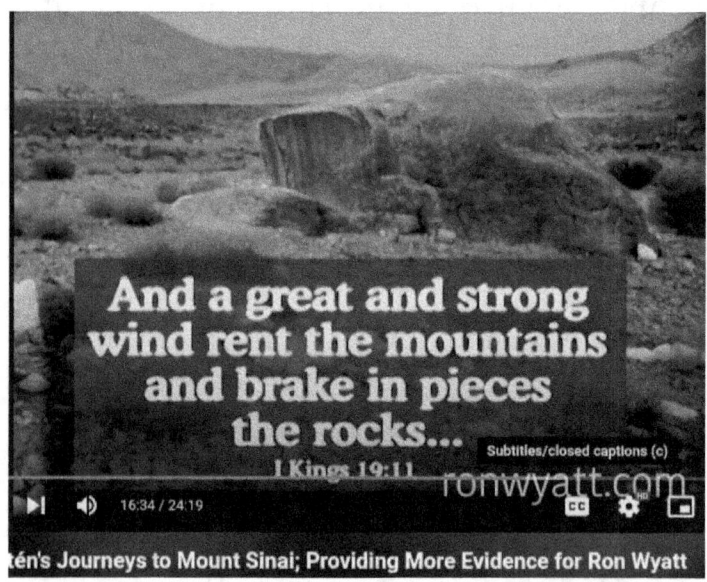

©Viveka Ponten, Split Boulders Near Real Mt. Sinai

# Timothy Mahoney

*Patterns of Evidence Film Series*

Filmmaker Timothy Mahoney has produced several documentaries on The Exodus. The first was released in 2009 and is titled *Exodus Conspiracy*. The second was released **in theaters** in 2015 and is called *Patterns of Evidence: The Exodus*.

He then made a two-part documentary called *Journey To Mount Sinai* and a second two-part series called *The Red Sea Miracle*. All of these provide evidence for the true Mt. Sinai being in Arabia and the actual Red Sea crossing being in the Gulf of Aqaba.[7]

# Ron Wyatt

**Ron Wyatt:** This is one of a matched pair of **columns set up at the crossing site** for the Habiru led by Moses (or Musa) across the Sea. The other one is on the opposite shore. The inscription tells that it was set up by order of King Solomon and it mentions that Pharaoh and his army were drowned by God in the waters here.[8]

Ron Wyatt (1933-1999) first visited the Red Sea crossing site at Nuweiba in 1978.

We didn't fully understand the importance of this column until a few years later—we did recognize that it was definitely not of Egyptian style. But in 1984, when we were imprisoned in Saudi Arabia, our captors, in an effort to verify our story that we believed Mt. Sinai was there and that "Musa" (Moses) led the people across the sea to their country, had me take them to the beach where they arrived after passing through the sea. I directed them to the spot in a helicopter. Landing here, I found another column—identical to the one on the opposite shore—except this one had the inscriptions intact.

Noting carefully the **Phoenician (Archaic Hebrew) letters**, we were later able to have it translated. It contained the words: **Mizraim (Egypt); Solomon; Edom; death; Pharaoh; Moses; and Yahweh.** From this, we knew that **King Solomon had erected these columns in honor** of **Yahweh** and dedicated them to the **miracle of the crossing of the sea**. And, that column possibly saved my sons' and my lives—it proved what I had been telling my Saudi jailers!

This year, we discovered that the Saudis have removed the column on their beach from its original location—they have sunk a large marker in concrete where it was located—and we are trying to locate it in their Antiquities files. But we have documented the solitary marker, sunk into the ground in concrete, on the beach, just down from the remains of the ancient fortress we believe was Baalzephon.⁹

Wyatt found chariot debris from Pharaoh's army:

> We will begin with the **chariot wheels** that Ron and the boys found in the Gulf of Aqaba. In 1978, on their first dive at the site, they found these chariot remains. Like Noah's Ark, these were not in perfect condition and required careful examination to see exactly what they were. They were covered in coral, which made it difficult to see them clearly, but it appears that the coral was the agent the Lord used to preserve them. They found numerous wheels—**some were still on their axles**, and some were off. They found **chariot cabs** without the wheels...They found several **6-spoked wheels**, as well as an **8-spoked wheel**. And finally, in 1988, Ron found the **4-spoked gold chariot wheel**...
>
> The significance of these wheels is of extreme importance to the dating of the Exodus and determining which dynasty was involved. Back in the late 70's, Ron actually retrieved a hub of a wheel which had the remains of 8 spokes radiating outward from it. **He took this to Cairo, to the office of Nassif Mohammed Hassan**, the director of Antiquities whom Ron had been working with. Mr. Hassan examined it and immediately **pronounced it to be of the 18th Dynasty of ancient Egypt**.¹⁰

All other researchers came *after* Ron Wyatt, yet not all acknowledged his work. Dr. Kim was driven to confirm Wyatt's statements, which he succeeded in doing. For more information on the discoveries of Ron Wyatt, watch this video: "Exodus to the Red Sea – the Discoveries of Ron Wyatt, *Vimeo*, Jul 1, 2015, https://vimeo.com/132387821.

## Summary

God meant for His defining event and its associated miracles to have evidence that stood the test of time. The Saudi Government is now allowing tourists to visit the real Mt. Sinai.

There are plenty of videos on YouTube with high-quality drone footage. It's now time for the world to know that Moses' account was genuine.

## Notes

1. Hershel Shanks, *Frank Moore Cross: Conversations With A Bible Scholar*, 1994, p. 13.
2. Bk.II, ch.12:1; Bk.III, ch.5:1.
3. Glen A. Fritz, *The Lost Sea of the Exodus: A Modern Geographical Analysis*, 2006, p. xiii.
4. "Where is the real Red Sea crossing site? Road To Sinai - Part 1 - The Crossing," *YouTube*, Jan 26, 2016, and "Is Mt Sinai in Saudi? Dr Kim's Amazing Testimony - Road to Sinai - Part II," *YouTube*, Sep 22, 2017.
5. "Is Mt Sinai in Saudi? Dr Kim's Amazing Testimony - Road to Sinai - Part II," *YouTube*, Sep 22, 2017.

6. "Viveka Pontén's Journeys to Mount Sinai; Providing More Evidence for Ron Wyatt," *YouTube*, Apr 21, 2021. It's also her view this is where Paul went after his conversion.
7. https://www.patternsofevidence.com/films/.
8. "Important Update on the Column on the Nuweiba Beach!!!," *YouTube*, Nov 17, 2024.
9. Ron Wyatt, "The Route of The Exodus Journeys- Part I," *Newsletter*, January, 1993, https://www.ronwyatt.com/red_sea_crossing.
10. Mary Nell Wyatt, "The Chariot Wheels in the Gulf of Aqaba, or Red Sea," *Newsletter*, April, 1993, https://www.ronwyatt.com/exodus_pt_2-_chariot_wheels.

# A PROPHET

The following Type is perhaps the most important because it pertains to Our Lord and His return. Moses was a Type of Our Lord. We can thank two people for clarifying this and its meaning: Moses, who gave the prophecy, and Peter, who framed it and restated it.

## THE PROPHECY

15 **The Lord thy God will raise up unto thee a Prophet** from the midst of thee, of thy brethren, **like unto me**; unto him ye shall hearken;
16 According to all that thou desiredst of the Lord thy God in Horeb in the day of the assembly, saying, Let me not hear again the voice of the Lord my God, neither let me see this great fire any more, that I die not.
17 And the Lord said unto me, They have well spoken that which they have spoken.
18 **I will raise them up a Prophet from among their brethren, like unto thee, and will put my words in his mouth; and he shall speak unto them all that I shall command him.**
19 And it shall come to pass, that whosoever will not hearken unto my words which he shall speak in my name, I will require it of him. (Deuteronomy 18)

# FRAMED & RESTATED

Peter cited Moses' prophecy within a post-mortality context, *before* The Millennium, with a different ending.

> 19 Repent ye therefore, and be converted, that your sins may be blotted out, when the **times of refreshing shall come from the presence of the Lord (a)**;
> 20 And **he shall send Jesus Christ, which before was preached unto you (b)**:
> 21 Whom the Heaven must receive until the **times of restitution of all things (c)**, which God hath spoken by the mouth of all his holy prophets since the world began.
> 22 **For Moses truly said unto the fathers, A prophet shall the Lord your God raise up unto you of your brethren, like unto me; him shall ye hear in all things whatsoever he shall say unto you.**
> 23 And it shall come to pass, that **every soul, which will not hear that prophet, SHALL BE DESTROYED (d) from among the people.** (Acts 3)

## Points

### a) Times of Refreshing

This statement is significant because it does not refer to the *Second Coming* of Our Lord but to a time *before* that. What word better describes this than "refreshing?" Note that this refreshing comes from Our Lord's "presence."

There have been different revivals and outpourings of The Holy Spirit, but those originated on Earth, where The Holy Spirit resides. This prophesied *refreshing* will come directly from the presence of Our Lord.

**b) Send Jesus Christ**

If we had not had this second part of the prophecy, we might have been uncertain about how the Times of Refreshing would come about. The prophecy plainly states that Our Lord will come. However, the idea that Our Lord will come twice may seem odd to some.

Many individuals have met Our Lord in modern times. A small group met Our Lord up close back then: Moses, Aaron, Nadab, Abihu, and seventy of the Elders of Israel. They will be the Type for those who have met Our Lord in modern times.

> 9 Then went up **Moses, and Aaron, Nadab, and Abihu, and seventy of the elders of Israel**:
> 10 And **they saw the God of Israel**: and there was under his feet as it were a paved work of a sapphire stone, and as it were the body of Heaven in his clearness.
> 11 And upon the nobles of the children of Israel he laid not his hand: also they saw God, and did eat and drink. (Exodus 24)

> 30 And **then shall appear the sign of the Son of man in Heaven**: and then shall all the tribes of the Earth mourn, and they shall see the Son of man coming in the clouds of Heaven with power and great glory.
> 31 And he shall **send his angels with a great sound of a trumpet, and they shall gather together his elect** from the four winds, from one end of Heaven to the other. (Matthew 24)

> 20 **Behold, I stand at the door, and knock**: if any man hear my voice, and open the door, **I will come in to him, and will sup with him**, and he with me. (Revelation 3)

## c) Times of Restitution

The "Times of Restitution" will restore Truth after the Apostasy.

> 3 Let no man deceive you by any means: for that day shall not come, except there come **a falling away first**, and that man of sin be revealed, the son of perdition; (2 Thessalonians 2)

## d) Destroy

The "destroy" part of this *Type* was absent from Our Lord's ministry. No one was threatened with death if they rejected His teachings. The Antichrist will now fulfill this.

# GOD

What happened on Mt. Sinai is a unique part of the account of Moses and the children of Israel as has already been established. The details provided by Moses are quite specific and worthy of our attention as they relate to the nature of God. Moses was commanded to bring the people to the desert of Sinai.

> 1 In the third month, when the children of Israel were gone forth out of the land of Egypt, the same day came they into the **wilderness of Sinai**.
> 2 For they were departed from Rephidim, and were come to the **desert of Sinai**, and had pitched in the wilderness; and there **Israel camped before the mount**. (Exodus 19)

The following morning, God came down on Mt. Sinai in front of the eyes of all the people.

> 16 And it came to pass on the third day in the morning, that **there were THUNDERS and LIGHTNINGS, and a thick cloud upon the mount, and the voice of the TRUMPET EXCEEDING LOUD; so that all the people that was in the camp trembled.**
> 17 And Moses brought forth the people out of the camp to meet with God; and they stood at the nether part of the mount.
> 18 And **mount Sinai was altogether on a**

> smoke, because the Lord descended upon it in FIRE: and the SMOKE thereof ascended as the SMOKE of a FURNACE, and the WHOLE MOUNT QUAKED GREATLY.
> 19 And when the **voice of the TRUMPET sounded LONG, and waxed LOUDER and LOUDER,** Moses spake, and God answered him by a voice. (Exodus 19)

Once God was upon the mount, He then spoke. What did God say? He gave the *Ten Commandments*.

> 1 And **God spake all these words**, saying,
> 2 I am the Lord thy God, which have brought thee out of the land of Egypt, out of the house of bondage.
> 3 **Thou shalt have no other gods before me...**
> (Exodus 20)

The voice of God was so terrifying to the children of Israel that they begged Moses to have God speak to him alone and then relay the messages back to them; otherwise, they feared they would perish.

> 18 And all the people saw the **thunderings**, and the **lightnings**, and the noise of the **trumpet**, and the mountain **smoking**: and when the people saw it, they removed, and stood afar off.
> 19 And they said unto Moses, **Speak thou with us, and we will hear: but let not God speak**

**with us, lest we die.**
20 And Moses said unto the people, Fear not: for God is come to prove you, and that his fear may be before your faces, that ye sin not.
21 And the people stood afar off, and Moses drew near unto the thick darkness where God was.
22 And the Lord said unto Moses, Thus thou shalt say unto the children of Israel, Ye have seen that I have talked with you from Heaven... (Exodus 20)

God gave Moses additional commandments, which can be found in the chapters that follow that account. In addition to the commandments, Moses received promises of protection.

20 Behold, **I SEND AN ANGEL BEFORE THEE**, to keep thee in the way, and to bring thee into the place which I have prepared.
21 Beware of him, and obey his voice, provoke him not; for he will not pardon your transgressions: for my name is in him.
22 But if thou shalt indeed obey his voice, and do all that I speak; then **I will be an enemy unto thine enemies, and an adversary unto thine adversaries**.
23 For **MINE ANGEL SHALL GO BEFORE THEE**, and bring thee in unto the Amorites, and the Hittites, and the Perizzites, and the Canaanites, the Hivites, and the Jebusites: and I will cut them off.
24 Thou shalt not bow down to their gods, nor

serve them, nor do after their works: but thou shalt utterly overthrow them, and quite break down their images.

And promises of blessings in a new land just for the Israelites.

25 And ye shall serve the Lord your God, and he shall **bless thy BREAD**, and **thy WATER;** and I will **take SICKNESS AWAY** from the midst of thee.
26 There shall nothing cast their young, **nor be barren**, **IN THY LAND**: the number of thy days I will fulfil.
27 I will send my fear before thee, and will destroy all the people to whom thou shalt come, and I will make all thine enemies turn their backs unto thee.
28 And **I will send hornets before thee**, which shall drive out the Hivite, the Canaanite, and the Hittite, from before thee.
29 I will not drive them out from before thee in one year; lest the land become desolate, and the beast of the field multiply against thee.
30 By little and little **I will drive them out from before thee, until thou be increased, and inherit the land**.
31 And I will set thy bounds from the Red sea even unto the sea of the Philistines, and from the desert unto the river: for **I will deliver the inhabitants of the land into your hand; and thou shalt drive them out before thee**. (Exodus 23)

Moses repeated these things to the children of Israel, and they agreed to abide by God's requirements.

> 3 And Moses came and told the people all the words of the Lord, and all the judgments: and all the people answered with one voice, and said, **All the words which the Lord hath said WILL WE DO.**
> 17 And **the sight of the glory of the Lord was like DEVOURING FIRe on the top of the mount in the eyes of the children of Israel.** (Exodus 24)

Based on this account, who was God? God was a devouring fire surrounded by a cloud of thunder, lightning, and smoke that caused the entire Mt. Sinai to quake.

He was accompanied by a trumpet that grew louder and louder, causing the people to tremble.

When God spoke, it caused such terror that the people thought they were going to die.

**Details of God**

- Glory
- Devouring fire
- Thunder
- Lightning
- Smoke
- Earthquake
- Trumpet

God | 137

- People trembled
- God spoke

## AT OTHER TIMES

God manifested Himself to the children of Israel as they journeyed.

> 21 And the **Lord went before them by day in a pillar of a cloud**, to lead them the way; and **by night in a pillar of fire, to give them light**; to go by day and night:
> 22 He took not away the **pillar of the cloud by day**, nor the **pillar of fire by night**, from before the people. (Exodus 13)

He protected them from the approaching Egyptian army.

> 19 And the **angel of God**, which went before the camp of Israel, removed and went behind them; and the **pillar of the cloud** went from before their face, and stood behind them:
> 20 And it came between the camp of the Egyptians and the camp of Israel; and **it was a cloud and darkness to them, but it gave light by night to these**: so that the one came not near the other all the night.
> 24 And it came to pass, that in the morning watch the **Lord looked unto the host of the Egyptians through the pillar of fire and of the cloud**, and troubled the host of the Egyptians (Exodus 14)

As they traveled toward the wilderness of Sinai, this is what they saw:

> 10 And it came to pass, as Aaron spake unto the whole congregation of the children of Israel, that they looked toward the wilderness, and, behold, **the glory of the Lord appeared in the cloud.** (Exodus 16)

At the Tabernacle of the Congregation,

> 7 And Moses took the tabernacle, and pitched it without the camp, afar off from the camp, and called it the **Tabernacle of the congregation**. And it came to pass, that **every one which sought the Lord went out unto the tabernacle of the congregation**, which was without the camp.
> 8 And it came to pass, when Moses went out unto the tabernacle, that all the people rose up, and stood every man at his tent door, and looked after Moses, until he was gone into the tabernacle.
> 9 And it came to pass, as Moses entered into the tabernacle, **the cloudy pillar descended, and stood at the door of the tabernacle, and the Lord talked with Moses**.
> 10 And all the people saw the cloudy pillar stand at the tabernacle door: and all the people rose up and worshipped, every man in his tent door.
> 11 And **the Lord spake unto Moses face to face, as a man speaketh unto his friend**. (Exodus 33; Num. 12:5,14:14; Deut. 33:15)

15 And **on the day that the tabernacle was reared up the cloud covered the tabernacle**, namely, the tent of the testimony: and **at even there was upon the tabernacle as it were the appearance of fire**, until the morning.
16 **So it was alway: the cloud covered it by day, and the appearance of fire by night.**
21 And so it was, when the cloud abode from even unto the morning, and that the cloud was taken up in the morning, then they journeyed: whether it was by day or by night that the cloud was taken up, they journeyed.
22 Or whether it were two days, or a month, or a year, that the cloud tarried upon the tabernacle, remaining thereon, the children of Israel abode in their tents, and journeyed not: but when it was taken up, they journeyed. (Numbers 9; Neh. 9:12,19; Ps. 99:7)

**Details About God**

- Pillar of a cloud
- Pillar of fire
- Cloudy pillar
- Cloud
- Fire

## OTHER PEOPLE

These are the accounts of other people who saw God upon His throne.

### Elders

9 Then went up Moses, and **Aaron**, **Nadab**, and **Abihu**, and **seventy of the elders** of Israel:
10 And they **saw the God of Israel: and there was under his feet as it were a paved work of a sapphire stone, and as it were the body of Heaven in his clearness.** (Exodus 24)

### Micaiah

18 Again he said, Therefore hear the word of the Lord; **I saw the Lord sitting upon his throne, and all the host of Heaven** standing on his right hand and on his left. (2 Chronicles 18)

### Ezekiel

26 And above the firmament that was over their heads was the likeness of a throne, as the appearance of a sapphire stone: and **upon the likeness of the throne was the likeness as the appearance of a man above upon it.**
27 And I saw as the colour of amber, as the appearance of **fire round about within it**, from the appearance of his loins even upward, and from the appearance of his loins even downward, I saw as it were the appearance of **fire**, and it **had brightness round about**.
28 As the appearance of the bow that is in the cloud in the day of rain, so was the appearance of the brightness round about. This was the appearance of the likeness of the **glory of the**

**Lord**. And when I saw it, I fell upon my face, and I heard a voice of one that spake. (Ezekiel 1)

## Isaiah

1 In the year that king Uzziah died **I saw also the Lord sitting upon a throne**, high and lifted up, and **his train filled the temple**.
2 Above it stood the seraphims: each one had six wings; with twain he covered his face, and with twain he covered his feet, and with twain he did fly.
3 And one cried unto another, and said, Holy, holy, holy, is the Lord of hosts: the whole Earth is full of his glory.
4 And the posts of the door moved at the voice of him that cried, and the **house was filled with smoke**. (Isaiah 6)

## Stephen

55 But he, being full of the Holy Ghost, looked up steadfastly into Heaven, and **saw the glory of God**, and Jesus standing on the right hand of God,
56 And said, Behold, I see the Heavens opened, and the Son of man standing on the right hand of God. (Acts 7)

## John

1 After this I looked, and, behold, a door was opened in Heaven: and the first voice which

I heard was as it were of a **trumpet** talking with me; which said, Come up hither, and I will shew thee things which must be hereafter.
2 And immediately I was in the spirit: and, behold, **a throne was set in Heaven, and one sat on the throne**.
5 And **out of the throne proceeded lightnings and thunderings and voices**: (Revelation 4)

**Details About God**

- Throne
- Paved work of a sapphire
- Body of Heaven
- Host of Heaven
- Fire round about within
- Brightness all around
- Glory
- His train filled the temple
- Smoke
- Lightnings, thunders, voices

## OTHER EVENTS

These are other events when God manifested Himself similarly to Moses and the children of Israel.

**Baptism of Jesus**

16 And Jesus, when he was **baptized**, went up straightway out of the water: and, lo, the

**Heavens were opened** unto him, and he saw the **Spirit of God** descending like a dove, and **lighting upon him:**
17 And lo a **voice from Heaven**, saying, This is my beloved Son, in whom I am well pleased. (Matthew 3)

## Transfiguration of Jesus

5 While he yet spake, behold, a **bright cloud overshadowed them:** and behold a **voice out of the cloud**, which said, This is my beloved Son, in whom I am well pleased; hear ye him. (Matthew 17)

16 For we have not followed cunningly devised fables, when we made known unto you the **power** and coming of our Lord Jesus Christ, but were eyewitnesses of his **majesty**.
17 For he received from God the Father honour and glory, **when there came such a voice to him from the excellent glory**, This is my beloved Son, in whom I am well pleased.
18 And this voice which **came from Heaven** we heard, when we were with him in the holy mount. (2 Peter 1)

## Ascension of Jesus

9 And when he had spoken these things, while they beheld, he was **taken up**; and a **cloud received him out of their sight**.
10 And while they looked steadfastly toward Heaven as he went up, behold, two men stood

by them in white apparel;
11 Which also said, Ye men of Galilee, why stand ye gazing up into Heaven? this same Jesus, which is taken up from you into Heaven, **shall so come in like manner** as ye have seen him go into Heaven. (Acts 1)

### Jesus Appeared to Paul

3 And as he journeyed, he came near Damascus: and suddenly there **shined round about him a light from Heaven:**
4 And he fell to the Earth, and heard a **voice** saying unto him, Saul, Saul, why persecutest thou me?
9 And he was three days without sight, and neither did eat nor drink. (Acts 9)

### Details About God

- Voice from Heaven
- Bright cloud
- Voice from cloud
- Cloud received Him
- Light from Heaven
- Voice

## OTHER MENTIONS

Here are other mentions regarding what happened to Moses and the children of Israel.

5 The **mountains melted** from before the

Lord, even that Sinai from before the Lord God of Israel. (Judges 5)

5 The **mountains quake** at him, and the **hills melt**, and the **Earth is burned at his presence**, yea, the world, and all that dwell therein. (Nahum 1)

8 The **Earth shook, the Heavens also dropped at the presence of God**: even **Sinai itself was moved at the presence of God**, the God of Israel. (Psalms 68)

18 The voice of thy **thunder** was in the Heaven: the **lightnings** lightened the world: the **Earth trembled and shook**. (Psalms 77)

1 The Lord reigneth; let the Earth rejoice; let the multitude of isles be glad thereof.
2 **Clouds** and **darkness** are round about him: righteousness and judgment are the habitation of his throne.
3 A **fire** goeth before him, and burneth up his enemies round about.
4 His **lightnings** enlightened the world: the **Earth** saw, and **trembled**.
5 The **hills melted** like wax at the **presence of the Lord**, at the presence of the Lord of the whole Earth.
6 The Heavens declare his righteousness, and all the people see his **glory**. (Psalms 97)

12 Moreover thou leddest them in the day by a **cloudy pillar**; and in the night by a **pillar of fire**, to give them light in the way wherein they

should go.
13 Thou **camest down also upon mount Sinai**, and **spakest with them from Heaven**, and gavest them right judgments, and true laws, good statutes and commandments: (Nehemiah 9)

**Details About God**

- Mountains melted
- Mountains quake
- Hills melt
- Earth shook
- Heavens dropped
- Sinai moved
- Thunder, lightning, Earth trembled and shook
- Clouds, darkness, fire, lightning, Earth trembled, hills melted, glory
- Cloudy pillar, pillar of fire, came down on Mt. Sinai, spake from Heaven

## PROPHECIES

Here's a list of prophecies that talk about God coming to Earth.

10 Enter into the rock, and hide thee in the dust, for fear of the Lord, and **for the glory of his majesty**.
11 The lofty looks of man shall be humbled, and the haughtiness of men shall be bowed down, and the Lord alone shall be exalted in that day.

12 For the day of the Lord of hosts **shall be upon every one** that is proud and lofty, and upon every one that is lifted up; and he shall be brought low: (Isaiah 2)

10 **Enter into the rock, and hide** thee in the dust, for fear of the LORD, and **for the glory of his majesty.**
11 The **lofty** looks of man shall be humbled, and the **haughtiness** of men shall be **bowed down**, and the LORD alone shall be exalted in that day.
12 For the **day of the LORD of hosts** shall be upon every one that is proud and lofty, and upon every one that is lifted up; and he shall be brought low:
19 And **they shall go into the holes of the rocks, and into the caves of the Earth, for fear of the LORD, and for the glory of his majesty, when he ariseth to shake terribly the Earth.**
20 In that day a man shall cast his idols of silver, and his idols of gold, which they made each one for himself to worship, to the moles and to the bats;
21 To go into the clefts of the rocks, and into the tops of the ragged rocks, **for fear of the LORD, and for the glory of his majesty, when he ariseth to shake terribly the Earth.** (Isaiah 2)

5 And the LORD will create upon every dwelling place of mount Zion, and upon her assemblies, **a cloud and smoke by day, and the**

shining of a flaming fire by night: for upon all the **glory** shall be a **defence**.
6 And there shall be a **tabernacle for a shadow** in the daytime from the heat, and for a **place of refuge**, and for a **covert from storm and from rain**. (Isaiah 4)

1 The burden of Egypt. Behold, the **LORD rideth upon a swift cloud**, and shall come into Egypt: and the **idols** of Egypt shall be **moved at his presence**, and the **heart of Egypt shall melt in the midst of it**. (Isaiah 19)

13 I saw in the night visions, and, behold, one like the **Son of man came with the clouds of Heaven**, and came to the Ancient of days, and they brought him near before him.
14 And there was given him dominion, and glory, and a kingdom, that all people, nations, and languages, should serve him: his dominion is an everlasting dominion, which shall not pass away, and his kingdom that which shall not be destroyed. (Daniel 7)

1 Blow ye the trumpet in Zion, and sound an alarm in my holy mountain: let all the inhabitants of the land tremble: for the **day of the LORD cometh**, for it is nigh at hand;
2 A day of darkness and of gloominess, **a day of clouds and of thick darkness, as the morning spread upon the mountains**: (Joel 2)

27 For **as the lightning cometh out of the east**, and shineth even unto the west; so shall also

the **coming of the Son of man** be.

28 For wheresoever the carcase is, **there will the eagles be gathered together.**

29 Immediately after the tribulation of those days shall the sun be darkened, and the moon shall not give her light, and the stars shall fall from Heaven, and the **powers of the Heavens shall be shaken:**

30 And then shall **appear the SIGN OF THE SON OF MAN IN HEAVEN**: and then shall all the **tribes of the Earth mourn**, and **they shall see the Son of man coming in the clouds of Heaven with power and great glory.**

31 And he shall send his angels with a **great sound of a trumpet**, and they shall **gather together his elect** from the four winds, from one end of Heaven to the other. (Matthew 24)

26 And then shall they **see the Son of man coming in the clouds** with **great power** and **glory**. (Mark 13)

25 And there shall be **signs** in the sun, and in the moon, and **in the stars**; and upon the **Earth distress** of nations, with perplexity; the **sea and the waves roaring;**

26 **Men's hearts failing them for fear**, and for looking after those **things which are coming** on the Earth: for the **powers of Heaven shall be shaken.**

27 And then shall they **see the Son of man coming in a cloud with power and great glory.**

28 And when these things begin to come to

pass, then look up, and lift up your heads; for **your redemption draweth nigh.** (Luke 21)

9 And when he had spoken these things, while they beheld, **he was taken up; and a cloud received him out of their sight.**
10 And while they looked stedfastly toward Heaven as he went up, behold, two men stood by them in white apparel;
11 Which also said, Ye men of Galilee, why stand ye gazing up into Heaven? this same Jesus, which is taken up from you into Heaven, **shall so come in like manner as ye have seen him go into Heaven.** (Acts 1)

16 For the Lord himself shall **descend from Heaven with a shout**, with the **voice of the archangel**, and with the **trump of God**: and the **dead in Christ shall rise** first:
17 Then **we which are alive and remain shall be caught up together with them in the clouds, to meet the Lord in the air:** and so shall we ever be with the Lord. (1 Thessalonians 4)

7 Behold, **he cometh with clouds; and every eye shall see him**, and they also which pierced him: and **all kindreds of the Earth shall wail because of him.** Even so, Amen. (Revelation 1)

12 And I beheld when he had opened the sixth seal, and, lo, there was a **great earthquake**; and the sun became black as sackcloth of hair, and the moon became as blood;

13 And the **stars of Heaven fell unto the Earth**, even as a fig tree casteth her untimely figs, when she is shaken of a mighty wind.

14 And the **Heaven departed as a scroll** when it is rolled together; and **every mountain and island were moved out of their places.**

15 And the **kings** of the Earth, and the **great men**, and the **rich men**, and the **chief captains**, and the **mighty men**, and every **bondman**, and every **free man**, **hid themselves** in the dens and in the rocks of the mountains;

16 And said to the mountains and rocks, Fall on us, and **hide us from the face of him that sitteth on the throne, and from the wrath of the Lamb:**

17 For the **great day** of his wrath is come; and who shall be able to stand? (Revelation 6)

## Details About God

- Glory upon everyone
- Glory of His majesty arises, shakes the Earth terribly
- Cloud and smoke by day, and the shining of a flaming fire by night
- Rideth on a swift cloud, idols moved at His presence, shall melt
- Son of man with the clouds of Heaven
- Day of the Lord, a day of clouds and thick darkness
- Like lightning, the coming of the Son of Man, powers of Heaven shaken, appear The Sign of

the Son of Man, see Son of man in clouds of Heaven, power, great glory, great trumpet, gather the elect
- See the Son of man, in clouds, great power, and glory
- Sea and waves roaring, powers in Heaven shaken, see Son of man coming, cloud, power, great glory, redemption draws nigh
- Come in a cloud
- Descend, shout, archangel, trump of God, caught up in clouds, be with Lord
- Comes with clouds, everyone sees
- Earthquake, stars fall, Heaven unrolls, mountains and islands move, people hide

## CONTEMPORARY ACCOUNTS

The following is a selection of contemporary accounts by people who visited Heaven and saw God upon His throne.

### Richard Sigmund

> There were millions multiplied by millions of people prostrate on their faces toward the Throne of God, which somehow faced every direction at the same time. **The Throne looked like it was twenty-five miles tall**. From any part of Heaven, you can see the Throne of God.[1]
>
> From this distance, I could tell that there was a Being on the Throne. But **He was cov-**

**ered with a cloud of glory that radiated from Him: an all-consuming, enfolding fire that was the glory of God Himself. He dwelt in a fire of glory.** The fire must have been the same thing Moses saw in the burning bush. Whatever it was, it surrounded the Being on the Throne.[2]

It was not as if I could see God clearly-I couldn't-but I could tell there was a Being on the Throne. Again, I never saw God plainly. I was not allowed to see Him except for one of His feet. **His foot seemed the size of the United States, and His toe looked the size of Tennessee.**[3]

**Jesse Duplantis**

I felt weaker and weaker as we approached the Throne room. It looked to me like millions of people were there.[4]

When the **light** from the Throne hit me I couldn't stand up.[5]

I looked up from the floor in the direction of the **overwhelming Light**, and I saw Him! I saw Elohim, Jehovah God, Yahweh sitting on the Throne! But I saw His feet—only His feet. The Light was so bright that came from Him, I couldn't see His face. Now I know why the Scripture says we can't see Jehovah's face and live—at least, I knew I couldn't! I had to keep looking down, the **Light was so intense**. But I looked again, and I saw the **lower part of His hand** resting on the arm of the Throne. **He is so big—you can't describe Him in a dimen-**

sion. **His hand is huge!** His **body**, the **form** of it, is sort of like **energy, spirit**.[6]

And that **power**, that **energy-like smoke** of God, covers all around the chair of the Throne itself...**There is smoke and power and noise, the place is noisy!**[7]

There was a **cloud** that looked like **smoke** going up from the Throne and I heard that **massive sound**, Whoosh! It was **power** like I've never experienced in my life.[8]

Jesus would walk in and out of the **power**, the **fire**, that massive amount of **energy**. When Jesus walked back into the energy, as He got closer, I would have to put my head down again, because I couldn't handle the **Light**. But that form of a Man as He walked toward that energy would transform back into Spirit.[9]

**Mary K. Baxter**

The angelic messenger took me to the throne of God. **I saw a huge cloud, a mist, and I saw an image of the Being in the cloud**. I could not see God's face, but I saw the **glory** of God and a rainbow over the throne. I heard the **voice** of God, and it sounded to me just as John described it: 'And I heard a voice from Heaven, as the voice of many waters, and as the voice of a great thunder.' (Revelation 14:2).[10]

I was allowed again to go before the throne of God and witness an awesome, exciting scene. **I could hear the sound of trumpets as I stood before the throne of God.**[11]

Then I saw a **cloud of glory filled with lightning, thunder, and voices**.[12]

## Oden Hetrick

Inside the jasper walls of the Temple or Most Holy Place is a courtyard garden. High above this enclosed garden, at the top of the beautiful walls is the **Throne of God**, characterized by a brilliant rainbow. This bright rainbow illumines the entire court with a perpetual profusion of prismatic hues. The space from the garden floor, to God's throne above, to the high walls round about is the seventh dimension. This hallowed habitation is the Holy of Holies of Heaven—the very Presence of the One true God who is the Temple of Heaven and the only Light in Celestial realms.[13]

It would seem that being close to the throne, we would be blinded by the light. But this is not the case. Because those who are allowed to come close to God on His throne are given brighter glory and this makes it possible for them to see God. It is God Himself who chooses who comes near Him. Jesus brought the light of life to men, and made it possible for saints to enter Heaven, and dwell in the light there.[14]

**The Throne of God appears to rest on a large white-with-light oval structure about 100 miles wide, 50 miles front to back, and 25 miles high**. But then again its size seems to vary greatly. It is difficult to describe; you will have to see it for yourself.[15]

That pattern was, and is the City of God. So Moses' Tabernacle had a Most Holy Place within a Holy Place where the priests would serve; and around these was a large area, or Outer Court for common people. **God's presence was manifested by a cloud of glory** in the Most Holy Place. So also as we approach God's abode in the sky, we come first to the large Outer Court or suburbs, then to the Holy Place, then to the Most Holy Place where God sits on His Throne.[16]

**Percy Collett**

This book is a true account of my walk in Heaven with Jesus. I saw the City Foursquare, the Throne of God, the River of Life, the Brazen Altar, and many Archangels, the Mansions, the Banqueting House, the Seats of Authority, the Eyes of Jesus which light up Heaven, Eternity, the Mother of Jesus, the Apostle Paul, Abraham, Elijah and other prophets.[17]

There was Heaven, in the midst of all the stars, **surrounded by fire, and lightning, and clouds.**[18]

**The GREAT THRONE OF GOD has a base over Two Thousand Miles Wide and Two Thousand Miles High which gives The Throne and The Altar Two Thousand Square Miles in all.**[19]

When I entered into the Gate, the First Reality that the three of us saw was THE GREAT WHITE THRONE OF GOD, which is not white as one would paint a wall with a flat or shiny white as only the Human Mind can understand. THE GREAT WHITE THRONE means the **Fire of GOD**, for GOD is a Consuming Fire and THE GREAT WHITE THRONE is so hot with so much Fire, that it is **WHITE hot**. And when an Earthly Furnace is brought to an Intensive Heat, It causes the Fire in the Furnace to become WHITE hot. The Whiteness of GOD's Throne has nothing to do with Color, White or Black; It is a **White Fire**.[20]

The Most High, The Almighty GOD, sits on Top of the Throne Two Thousand Miles above the Base; there sit GOD The Father and His Son.[21]

**The Throne of GOD has Power and Glory and Authority coming from it and all around it.**[22]

**GOD is a Spirit** and His Spirit extends out into the Everlasting, which has No End or No Beginning. Jesus, GOD's Son, can reveal Himself in His Heavenly Body to any Part of this Earth or to any Part of the Universe like His Father. Jesus is a Revelation of GOD. THE Holy Ghost is a Revelation of Jesus. This gives you the Revelation of the Triune Godhead.[23]

### Tony Kemp

My spirit left my body. I went to the throne of God, **which by the way is as big as a mountain.** God spoke to me. I wouldn't even lift up my head because the experience of God's presence and **glory** was just so great. I was literally at His feet.[24]

## Brian Simmons

Brian Simmons shared an experience when God's glory came into a meeting, which caught the church on fire.

> I got invited to speak at this beautiful church in Providence and I went and I said God give me the word, and He said, tell the congregation I'm going to send a coal of fire to this church, and I spoke it out three times. I was so impressed that I was to deliver that message. And the third time, the pastor and his wife jumped up and pointed over my head and said there are flames of fire coming out of the ceiling everybody leave right now. Two hundred and fifty plus people saw it. I felt it, it felt like the presence of God. There was smoke that filled the building. **There was an actual fire**, a true fire because twelve firemen had to come put it out...The insurance company had to spend tens of thousands of dollars to repair the damage.[25]

It's interesting to compare details about God's appearance on Mt. Sinai with prophecies about God coming to Earth, contemporary accounts of people who visited Heaven and saw God upon His throne, and Biblical accounts of those who saw God upon His throne. These descriptions confirm the validity of God in the account of Moses and the children of Israel.

But which God was it? God the Father, God the Son, or God the Holy Ghost?

## WHICH GOD?

Which God appeared to Moses and the children of Israel? Was it God the Father, God the Son, or God the Holy Ghost? This concept wasn't on my radar until I read this passage by Paul.

> 1 Moreover, brethren, I would not that ye should be ignorant, how that all our fathers were under the cloud, and all passed through the sea;
> 2 And were all baptized unto Moses in the cloud and in the sea;
> 3 And did all eat the same spiritual meat;
> 4 And did all drink the same spiritual drink: for **they drank of that spiritual Rock that followed them: and that Rock WAS CHRIST.** (1 Corinthians 10)

Indeed, I'm not the only one who wondered after reading that stanza if Our Lord was with the children of Israel, and if He was, by what name was He known?

### Paradox

There is an apparent paradox between the account

of Moses and the children of Israel "seeing God" and Bible verses that say "no one has seen God." It says no one has seen Him, and no one has "heard His voice" at any time.

> 18 **No man hath seen God at any time**; the only begotten Son, which is in the bosom of the Father, he hath declared him. (John 1)

> 37 And the Father himself, which hath sent me, hath borne witness of me. **Ye have neither heard his voice at any time, nor seen his shape.** (John 5)

> 12 **No man hath seen God at any time.** If we love one another, God dwelleth in us, and his love is perfected in us. (1 John 4)

> 9 Then went up Moses, and Aaron, Nadab, and Abihu, and seventy of the elders of Israel:
> 10 And **they saw the God of Israel**: (Exodus 24)

> 22 And the Lord said unto Moses, Thus thou shalt say unto the children of Israel, **Ye have seen that I have talked with you from Heaven.** (Exodus 20)

If Our Lord referred to God the Father as the one who was never before seen and whose voice was never heard, then perhaps it wasn't God the Father who came down on Sinai. Let's review other verses about God and see what we can learn.

## Judge

Who will judge the world, God the Father or God the Son?

> 25 Shall not the **Judge** of all the Earth do right? (Genesis 18)

> 22 For the Father judgeth no man, but hath committed **ALL JUDGMENT unto the Son**: (John 5)

## God

Was Jesus ever called "God" in the *New Testament*, or was it always just the "Son of God"?

> 8 But unto the Son he saith, **Thy throne, O God**, is for ever and ever: a sceptre of righteousness is the sceptre of thy kingdom. (Hebrews 1)

## Creator

The first chapter of John presents Jesus differently than the other three Gospels. It says Jesus is "God" and "Creator."

> 1 In the beginning was the Word, and the Word was with God, and **the Word was God**.
> 3 **ALL THINGS were MADE BY HIM**; and without him was not any thing made that was made. (John 1)

Other scriptures confirm Our Lord is *The Creator*.

> 15 Who is the image of the invisible God, the firstborn of every creature:
> 16 For **BY HIM were all things CREATED,** that are in Heaven, and that are in Earth, visible and invisible, whether they be thrones, or dominions, or principalities, or powers: **all things were created BY HIM, and for him**:
> 17 And he is before all things, and **BY HIM all things consist**. (Colossians 1)

> 2 Hath in these last days spoken unto us by his Son, whom he hath appointed heir of all things, **BY WHOM also he MADE the worlds**; (Hebrews 1)

> 10 For it became him, **for whom are all things**, and **BY WHOM are all things**, in bringing many sons unto glory, to make the captain of their salvation perfect through sufferings. (Hebrews 2)

So, Our Lord was the first thing God the Father created. After that, Our Lord created everything else. But that's not all. Our Lord also *sustains* all His creations and is inseparably related to them. Those realizations placed Our Lord in a whole new light. This means that Our Lord is *more* than ancient. It's hard to equate the thirty-three-year-old Savior who walked the Earth, bled, and died on the cross, with the God who created all things and is probably trillions of years old.

This understanding can help us appreciate God's condescension to become like us. What helped me to comprehend the arrangement between God the Father and God the Son is viewing Our Father as the *Master Architect* and Our Lord as the *Master Builder*.

## I AM

Perhaps the statement by Jesus that best solidified His place in the Bible for me was when He referred to Himself as "I AM," *which was the same name He used when He appeared to Moses and the children of Israel.*

> 58 Jesus said unto them, Verily, verily, I say unto you, Before Abraham was, **I AM**. (John 8)

> 14 And God said unto Moses, **I AM THAT I AM**: and he said, **Thus shalt thou say unto the children of Israel, I AM** hath sent me unto you. (Exodus 3)

The significance of this was driven home by *Bauscherp*, the translator of *The Original Aramaic New Testament in Plan English*. He said,

> One question many ask about the Aramaic text is, 'Are there major differences in this text compared to other translations? The answer is about 95% of the text is the same as other New Testaments, but the 5% difference is really interesting, significant and powerful 5%

content...Our Lord used the Aramaic phrase, '**Ena Na**', which signifies a Divine utterance in 97% of the places it is found in The Peshitta Old Testament—'**I am** the Lord your God', '**I am** the Lord who heals you', etc., in hundreds of references. **Our Lord used this phrase of Himself about thirty times**...This is a powerful testimony that **YESHUA CLAIMED TO BE GOD HIMSELF**...John's gospel has 25 instances of Jesus uttering these '**I AM**' statements.[26]

Because Aramaic is the language that Our Lord spoke (not Greek), it's curious why Bible students have pursued Greek exclusively to understand the New Testament. The Aramaic clarifies that Our Lord did not beat around the bush regarding who He was.

> 12 And Yeshua spoke again with them and he said: "**I AM THE LIVING GOD**, The Light of the world.
> 18 "**I AM THE LIVING GOD**, I who testify about myself, and my Father who has sent me has testified about Me."
> 24 "I said to you that you shall die in your sins, for unless you shall believe that **I AM THE LIVING GOD**, you shall die in your sins."
> 28 Yeshua spoke again to them: "When you have lifted up The Son of Man, then you shall know that **I AM THE LIVING GOD**, and I do nothing for my own pleasure, but just as my Father has taught me, so I am speaking.

56 "Abraham your father desired to see my day, and he saw it and rejoiced."
57 The Jews were saying to him, "You are not yet fifty years old, and you have seen Abraham?"
58 Yeshua said to them: "Timeless truth I speak to you: Before Abraham would exist, **I AM THE LIVING GOD**." (John 8 *Aramaic Plain English*)

3 Therefore Yehuda led a company also from the presence of the Chief Priests and the Pharisees. He led the guards and came there with torches and lamps and weapons.
4 But Yeshua, because he knew all these things had come upon him, went out and said to them, "Whom are you seeking?"
5 They were saying to him, "Yeshua the Nazarene." Yeshua said to them, "**I AM THE LIVING GOD**." But Yehuda the traitor was also standing with them.
6 And when Yeshua said to them, "**I AM THE LIVING GOD**", they went backward and fell to the ground.
7 Yeshua said again, "Whom are you seeking?" But they said, "Yeshua the Nazarene."
8 Yeshua said to them, "I have told you that **I AM THE LIVING GOD**, and if you are seeking me, let these men go." (John 18 *Aramaic Plain English*)

60 The High Priest stood up in the center and asked Yeshua, and he said, "Do you not answer? Why are these testifying against

you?"
61 But he was silent, and he did not answer him anything. And again, The High Priest asked him and said, "Are you The Messiah, The Son of The Blessed One?"
62 But Yeshua said to him, "**I AM THE LIVING GOD**, and you shall behold The Son of Man sitting at the right hand of Power and coming on the clouds of Heaven." (Mark 14 *Aramaic Plain English*)

It makes sense that Our Lord told His disciples they would be persecuted for His "name's sake."

12 But before all these, they shall lay their hands on you, and persecute you, delivering you up to the synagogues, and into prisons, being brought before kings and rulers for my **name's sake**.
17 And ye shall be hated of all men for my **name's sake**. (Luke 21)

Bauscherp put it like this,

> **'Metul Shemi' ('because of my name')** is such an important phrase, repeated in v. 17 and elsewhere as the cause of all the controversy and persecution against the church. What is His name and why all the persecution? His Name, according to The Peshitta, which every Believer must confess and to Which each was baptized is, **(MarYah Yeshua Meshikha)—'The Lord God Yeshua The Messiah'**. Paul would later write: **'No one can say Yeshua is Jehovah

**(LORD God) except by the Holy Spirit.'** Whosoever does not believe He is **Jehovah** God does not believe in Him. Whosoever has not confessed with his mouth '**The LORD God Yeshua**' should do so. The Holy Spirit alone can bring this home to the heart and soul and compel the mouth to confess it, as He did to Peter. Some day '<u>**Every knee shall bow and every tongue confess** that **Yeshua Meshikha is MarYah (The Lord God), to the glory of God The Father.**</u>' Phillip 2:11[27]

The original Aramaic places Our Lord in the proper light, in which He was always meant to be viewed. This perspective of Him matches with the God who appeared to Moses and the children of Israel at Mt. Sinai: The Almighty, Powerful God, who is the Creator of All, the Great I AM, or as Isaiah put it:

> 6 For unto us a **Child is born**, Unto us a **Son is given**; And the government will be upon His shoulder. And His name will be called **Wonderful, Counselor, Mighty God, Everlasting Father, Prince of Peace.** (Isaiah 9 NKJV)

That's the God we are to CONFESS with our mouths. The one we are to ACCEPT. The one who will JUDGE. The one who is RETURNING. The one to whom EVERY KNEE MUST BOW. What is the mission of The Holy Ghost? To testify of Jesus (Jn.15:26). But not any Jesus, the *full* Jesus, which correctly translated from the Aramaic is: "The Lord God Yeshua The Messiah."

## Notes

1. Richard Sigmund, *My Time In Heaven*, 2009, p. 106.
2. Ibid., p. 107.
3. Ibid., p. 109.
4. Jesse Duplantis, *Heaven - Close Encounters of the God Kind*, 1996, p. 111.
5. Ibid., p. 113.
6. Ibid., p. 115.
7. Ibid., p. 114.
8. Ibid., p. 115.
9. Ibid., p. 118.
10. Mary K. Baxter, *A Divine Revelation Of Heaven*, 1998, p. 37.
11. Ibid., p. 75.
12. Ibid., p. 76.
13. Oden Hetrick, *Inside the Gates of Heaven*, 2013, p. 82.
14. Ibid., p. 83.
15. Ibid., p. 84.
16. Ibid., p. 19.
17. Percy Collett, *I Walked In Heaven With Jesus*, 1986, Preface.
18. Ibid., p. 7.
19. Ibid., p. 43.
20. Ibid., p. 47.
21. Ibid., p. 48.
22. Ibid., p. 50.

23. Ibid., p. 51.
24. (*Sid Roth Transcript*, August 2, 2010, p. 6.
25. *Sid Roth Radio Interview*, Jan. 26, 2015, 28:44.
26. David Bauscherp, *The Original Aramaic New Testament in Plain English*, 2007, pp. 5-6.
27. Bauscherp, p. 125, emphasis his.

# GLORY

One of the most significant things we can expect to return is God's glory in its Shekinah form. I lightly touched on it in Chapter *Fiery Serpents*. For those unfamiliar with *The Shekinah*, it's the dwelling of the Divine Presence of God.

I could have never imagined that The Shekinah that accompanied the children of Israel and split the Rock in Horeb was a Type of what will occur on Temple Mount in our day. I'll insert the chapter "The Vision" from *Temple Mount 11:11 Horn of God*, to explain how It will come and what will happen.

## THE VISION

Recently, God's Spirit descended upon me again, but this time, I was transported into the future and shown the Dome of the Rock Shrine on Temple Mount in Jerusalem. There I beheld *The Shekinah of God* come down upon the Holy Mount and split the rock under the Dome in half, just like the Rock of Horeb, and water came gushing forth with such force that it destroyed the Shrine.

God's Spirit then led me to the following prophecy:

8 And it shall be in that day, that **living waters shall go out from Jerusalem**; half of them toward the former sea, and half of them

toward the hinder sea: **in summer and in winter shall it be**. (Zechariah 14)

After this, I observed The Shekinah move slightly north and east while still on the Mount where it stood.[1] I was informed that the Split Rock of Horeb foreshadowed this event, and that is why I was permitted to witness it, that I may testify of them both.

## The Shekinah

For those unfamiliar with the word *Shekinah*, it's the dwelling of the *Divine Presence* of God, such as occurred with the children of Israel (and at other times). Here are a few examples and prophecies about Its return:

> 21 And **the Lord went before them by day in a PILLAR OF A CLOUD**, to lead them the way; and **by night in a PILLAR OF FIRE, to GIVE THEM LIGHT**; to go by day and night:
> 22 He took not away the pillar of the cloud by day, nor the pillar of fire by night, from before the people. (Exodus 13)

> 10 And it came to pass, when the priests were come out of the holy place, that **THE CLOUD filled the house of the Lord**,
> 11 So that the priests could not stand to minister because of the **CLOUD: for the GLORY of the LORD had filled the house of the Lord**. (1 Kings 8)

13 And **I WILL DWELL among the children of Israel**, and **will not forsake my people Israel**. (1 Kings 6)

14 This is my rest for ever: **here will I DWELL; for I have desired it.** (Psalms 132)

4 And said unto him, Run, speak to this young man, saying, **Jerusalem shall be inhabited as towns without walls** for the multitude of men and cattle therein:
5 **For I**, saith the Lord, will be unto her a wall of fire round about, and **WILL BE THE GLORY IN THE MIDST OF HER**.
10 Sing and rejoice, O daughter of Zion: **for, lo, I come, and I WILL DWELL IN THE MIDST OF THEE, saith the Lord.**
11 And many nations shall be joined to the Lord in that day, and shall be my people: and **I WILL DWELL IN THE MIDST OF THEE**, and thou shalt know that the Lord of hosts hath sent me unto thee.
12 And **the Lord shall inherit Judah** his portion in the holy land, and **shall choose Jerusalem again.** (Zechariah 2)

Next, while I was still in God's Spirit, I saw the effect The Shekinah had on the inhabitants of Jerusalem and those who came to see it. In one area, I saw people *weeping* and *mourning*; in another, I saw *teeth gnashing*. Those who could endure it looked *into* The Shekinah and saw a figure within it. For them, it was clear this was Our Lord, Jesus Christ.

I then saw reporters asking people who had just come from seeing The Shekinah about their experience. The most common reply was:

> It's the Holy Presence of God; only the holy can look *into* it.

The Shekinah was not a commercial spectacle; it indeed was the Holy Presence of God, returning like God said it would. It will be the *first* of many End Time events to occur. Much repenting will happen as people reconcile themselves with the existence of God and Jesus Christ as the Messiah.

Gustave Doré, *God's Army Appears Overhead*

# People Will Come and Learn About God's Fire

After The Shekinah arrives, a greater interest will come in becoming more spiritual.

> 1 But in the last days it shall come to pass, that THE MOUNTAIN [Temple Mount] of the house of **the Lord shall be established in the top of the mountains [God's Holy Fire first]**, and it shall be exalted above the hills; and **PEOPLE SHALL FLOW UNTO IT [they will want to learn about Him]**.
> 2 And many nations shall come, and say, Come, and let us go up to the mountain of the Lord, and to the house of the God of Jacob; and **HE WILL TEACH US of his WAYS [how is God a fire?]**, and **we will WALK IN HIS PATHS [become more spiritually advanced]**: for the law shall go forth of Zion, and the word of the Lord from Jerusalem.
> 3 And he shall judge among many people, and **rebuke strong nations afar off [distant nations who care about tomorrow will desire to learn about this God and align with His will]**; and they shall beat their swords into plowshares, and their spears into pruninghooks: nation shall not lift up a sword against nation, neither shall they learn war any more. (Micah 4)

[End of Insert]

# GOD'S SPIRIT VS. HOLY GHOST

The final revival on Earth will differ from other times because the Spirit of God Our Father will increase exponentially and not more of The Holy Ghost.[2] For this reason, it's essential to understand what is different between the two.

First and foremost, God Our Father did not create a god greater than Himself. There's no gift, power, ability, or influence that The Holy Ghost has that Our Father lacks.

Secondly, we don't need to look outside ourselves for that mysterious "Holy Ghost" spirit when God's Spirit is *already* within us. It only needs to be "Quickened."

> 16 Know ye not that **ye are the TEMPLE of GOD**, and that the **SPIRIT of GOD DWELLETH IN YOU**? (1 Corinthians 3)

> 13 I give thee charge in the sight of **GOD, who QUICKENETH all things**, and before Christ Jesus, who before Pontius Pilate witnessed a good confession; (1 Timothy 6)

What happened to the apostles on the Day of Pentecost came from *without* and rested upon them:

> 1 And when the **day of Pentecost** was fully come, they were all with one accord in one place.
> 2 And suddenly **there came a sound from heaven as of a rushing mighty wind**, and it

filled all the house where they were sitting.
3 And there appeared unto them **cloven tongues like as of fire**, and it sat upon each of them.
4 And they were all **filled with the Holy Ghost**, and began to speak with other tongues, **as the Spirit gave them utterance**. (Acts 2)

Here's an example of God's Spirit becoming *Quickened* within.

13 And, behold, two of them went that same day to a village called Emmaus, which was from Jerusalem about threescore furlongs.
14 And they talked together of all these things which had happened.
15 And it came to pass, that, while they communed together and reasoned, **Jesus himself drew near**, and **went with them**.
16 But their eyes were holden that **they should not know him**.
17 And he said unto them, What manner of communications are these that ye have one to another, as ye walk, and are sad?
18 And the one of them, whose name was Cleopas, answering said unto him, Art thou only a stranger in Jerusalem, and hast not known the things which are come to pass there in these days?
19 And he said unto them, What things? And they said unto him, Concerning Jesus of Nazareth, which was a prophet mighty in deed and word before God and all the people:
20 And how the chief priests and our rulers

delivered him to be condemned to death, and have crucified him.

21 But we trusted that it had been he which should have redeemed Israel: and beside all this, to day is the third day since these things were done.

22 Yea, and certain women also of our company made us astonished, which were early at the sepulchre;

23 And when they found not his body, they came, saying, that they had also seen a vision of angels, which said that he was alive.

24 And certain of them which were with us went to the sepulchre, and found it even so as the women had said: but him they saw not.

25 Then he said unto them, O fools, and slow of heart to believe all that the prophets have spoken:

26 Ought not Christ to have suffered these things, and to enter into his glory?

27 And **beginning at Moses and all the prophets, he expounded unto them in all the scriptures** the things concerning himself.

28 And they drew nigh unto the village, whither they went: and he made as though he would have gone further.

29 But they constrained him, saying, Abide with us: for it is toward evening, and the day is far spent. And he went in to tarry with them.

30 And it came to pass, as he sat at meat with them, **he took bread, and blessed it, and brake, and gave to them.**

31 And **their eyes were opened**, and **THEY**

**KNEW HIM**; and he vanished out of their sight.
32 And they said one to another, **Did not our HEART BURN WITHIN US**, while he talked with us by the way, and **WHILE HE OPENED TO US THE SCRIPTURES**? (Luke 24)

Those who have experienced this liken it to *Spirit Nuclear Fusion.* This Spirit lies dormant within each of us and, if cultivated, can flow like a river. Because God is a *consuming fire* (Deut.4:24, 9:3; Heb.12:29), we can or should feel a *burning in the bosom* when His Spirit is Quickened within us, just like the disciples did. I say "should" because it depends on how much sin is in us, or how hardened our hearts are (Rom.2:5), or if we have become "past feeling" (Eph.4:19).

This understanding is not meant to negate the role of The Holy Ghost but rather to acknowledge its rightful place *after* using The Spirit of God that is *already* within us. The following verses that refer to becoming "Quickened" are quite enlightening.

> 105 **THY WORD is a lamp unto my feet, and a light unto my path**.
> 106 I have sworn, and I will perform it, that **I will keep thy righteous judgments**.
> 107 I am afflicted very much: **QUICKEN ME, O Lord, ACCORDING unto THY WORD**.
> 108 Accept, I beseech thee, the freewill offerings of my mouth, O Lord, and teach me thy judgments.
> 109 My soul is continually in my hand: yet **do I**

not forget thy law.
110 **The wicked have laid a snare for me: yet I erred not from THY PRECEPTS.**
111 Thy testimonies have I taken as an heritage for ever: for they are the rejoicing of my heart.
112 **I have inclined mine heart to perform thy statutes alway, even unto the end.** (Psalms 119)

153 Consider mine affliction, and deliver me: **for I do not forget thy law.**
154 Plead my cause, and deliver me: **QUICKEN ME ACCORDING to THY WORD.**
155 Salvation is far from the **wicked: for they seek not thy statutes.**
156 Great are thy tender mercies, O Lord: **QUICKEN ME according to thy judgments.**
157 **Many are my persecutors and mine enemies; yet do I not decline from thy testimonies.**
158 I beheld the transgressors, and was grieved; because **THEY KEPT NOT THY WORD.**
159 **CONSIDER HOW I LOVE THY PRECEPTS: QUICKEN ME, O Lord, ACCORDING TO THY LOVINGKINDNESS.**
160 **THY WORD IS TRUE** from the beginning: and every one of thy righteous judgments endureth for ever. (Psalms 119)

10 **Teach me to do thy will**; for thou art my God: **THY SPIRIT IS GOOD; lead me into the land of uprightness.**

11 **QUICKEN ME,** O Lord, **for thy name's sake: for thy righteousness' sake bring my soul out of trouble.** (Psalms 143)

## Formula

*God's Word => Quickens God's Spirit Already Within Us => Quickens Us*

For more information on this very important topic, see my book *Quickened Within – Mystery of the Inner Man*.

## Notes

1. For in-depth Shekinah discussions and references, see *Appendix: Shekinah References*.
2. We know this from Percy Collett's tape testimonies.

# DECEPTION

There was considerable spiritual deception going on in Egypt with their false gods, false religion, and false prophets, and a great deal of it followed the children of Israel when they left. In other words, the children of Israel did not live in a vacuum. The accounts of their rebellion after all that God did cannot be understood without this factor.

Why else would a people turn from their God after seeing His demonstrations of power, glory, and miracles on their behalf? It's not that they became spiritually lazy; they were *deceived* into replacing Him with a golden calf.

To help me comprehend why that happened, God opened my eyes to the Spirit World and revealed different modern ministries to me. I saw that their "tongues" (the Tongue of Devils), worship, "healings" (which are temporary), words of knowledge (Spirit of Divination, Acts 16:16), etc., traced to the Father of Lies or Man of Sin.

> 3 Let no man deceive you by any means: for that day shall not come, except **there come a falling away first**, and that **MAN of SIN be revealed**, the son of perdition;
> 4 Who opposeth and **exalteth himself** above all that is called God, or that is **worshipped;** so that **HE AS GOD sitteth in the temple of God [our bodies including corporate bodies]**,

**SHEWING HIMSELF THAT HE IS GOD.** (2 Thessalonians 2)

I was unaware that Satan could do what Paul said happened in his time.

> 13 For such are false apostles, deceitful workers, transforming themselves into the **APOSTLES of CHRIST**.
> 14 And no marvel; for **Satan himself is transformed into an ANGEL of LIGHT**.
> 15 Therefore **it is no great thing if his ministers also be transformed as the MINISTERS of RIGHTEOUSNESS**; whose end shall be according to their works. (2 Corinthians 11)

I was compelled to affirm that the deceiving spirits that plagued the children of Israel were active in Paul's day and are with us now. We're not just talking about good or bad angels. We must include the very competent yet prideful dead who thought they were too smart to believe in God. They refuse to return to Him for a life review and have set up "shop" one dimension over and meddle.

> 6 Or ever the **silver cord be loosed [connects spirit to the body]**, or the golden bowl be broken, or the pitcher be broken at the fountain, or the wheel broken at the cistern.
> 7 Then shall the dust return to the earth as it was: and **the spirit shall return unto God** who gave it. (Ecclesiastes 12)

Some percent even work for Satan and do his bidding among their living family and friends. The Spirit World is far more complex than most people understand, and spirits are far more active among religions, where people reach into the unknown to try and connect with angels, the Holy Ghost, etc.

I detail different types of deception in the following books.

- *Abomination of Desolation* – clears up misunderstandings about the Antichrist, a third Temple, the Man of Sin, and Abomination of Desolation prophecies.
- *Babylon: Then & Now* – identifies non-Biblical church practices and who the "whore of Babylon" is.
- *Before He Comes* – identifies three little-known prophecies that must happen before Our Lord returns.
- *Coming War in Heaven, The* – identifies deceivers of all types, including Extraterrestrials.
- *Joy-Filled Way, The* – teaches the true role of ministers and churches.
- *Quicken Within – Mystery of the Inner Man* – teaches the differences between the Holy Ghost and God's Spirit and how to quicken it safely.
- *Scotland* – has information on how and when the Catholic Church became corrupted.
- *Spirits Among Us* – teaches about the defiant dead and how to handle them.

# WEALTH TRANSFER

The transfer of wealth from the wicked to the righteous has been prophesied, and how it occurred for the Israelites is the final *Type* we will address.

## PROPHECIES

22 A good man leaveth an inheritance to his children's children: and **the wealth of the sinner is laid up for the just.** (Proverbs 13)

18 But thou shalt remember the Lord thy God: for **it is he that giveth thee power to get wealth, that he may establish his covenant** which he sware unto thy fathers, as it is this day. (Deuteronomy 8)

26 For God giveth to a man that is good in his sight wisdom, and knowledge, and joy: but to the sinner he giveth travail, to gather and to heap up, **that he may give to him that is good before God.** (Ecclesiastes 2)

24 **Then shalt thou lay up gold as dust**, and the gold of Ophir as the stones of the brooks.
25 Yea, the Almighty shall be thy defence, and **thou shalt have plenty of silver**.
26 For then shalt thou have thy delight in the Almighty, and shalt lift up thy face unto God. (Job 22)

16 Though he heap up silver as the dust, and prepare raiment as the clay;
17 He may prepare it, but **the just shall put it on, and the innocent shall divide the silver.** (Job 27)

## TYPE

We see with the Israelites a transfer of wealth from the wicked:

22 But every woman shall borrow of her neighbour, and of her that sojourneth in her house, **jewels of silver**, and **jewels of gold**, and **raiment:** and ye shall put them upon your sons, and upon your daughters; and **ye shall spoil the Egyptians.** (Exodus 3)

2 Speak now in the ears of the people, and let every man borrow of his neighbour, and every woman of her neighbour, jewels of silver, and jewels of gold.
3 And **the Lord gave the people favour in the sight of the Egyptians.** (Exodus 11)

35 And the children of Israel did according to the word of Moses; and **they borrowed** of the Egyptians **jewels of silver**, and **jewels of gold**, and **raiment:**
36 And **the Lord gave the people favour in the sight of the Egyptians**, so that they lent unto them such things as they required. And **they spoiled the Egyptians.** (Exodus 12)

They were allowed to take the spoils of the Egyptians and the cities they would later conquer.

9 And the children of Israel took all the women of Midian captives, and their little ones, and took the **spoil of all their cattle, and all their flocks, and all their goods.**
10 And they burnt all their cities wherein they dwelt, and all their goodly castles, with fire.
11 And **they took all the spoil, and all the prey, both of men and of beasts.**
12 And **they brought the captives, and the prey, and the spoil**, unto Moses, and Eleazar the priest, and unto the congregation of the children of Israel, unto the camp at the plains of Moab, which are by Jordan near Jericho. (Numbers 31)

35 Only the cattle we took for a prey unto ourselves, and the **spoil of the cities which we took.** (Deuteronomy 2)

7 But all the cattle, and the **spoil of the cities, we took for a prey to ourselves.** (Deuteronomy 3)

14 But the women, and the little ones, and the cattle, and all that is in the city, even **all the spoil thereof, shalt thou take unto thyself**; and thou shalt eat the spoil of thine enemies, which the Lord thy God hath given thee. (Deuteronomy 20)

In addition, there are promises of wealth in scripture that Prosperity Preachers are fond of using in their sermons. If taken together, i.e., the prophecies, promises, and the Israelite *Type*, we have what could be construed as a guaranteed financial windfall for the righteous in the coming days. There's just one caveat—arrogance.

## ARROGANCE

God warned Moses and the children of Israel against arrogance and told them not to forget their God and how they acquired their wealth.

> 11 **Beware that thou forget not the Lord thy God**, in not keeping his commandments, and his judgments, and his statutes, which I command thee this day:
> 12 Lest when thou hast eaten and art full, and hast built goodly houses, and dwelt therein;
> 13 And when thy herds and thy flocks multiply, and thy silver and thy gold is multiplied, and all that thou hast is multiplied;
> 14 **Then thine heart be lifted up, and thou forget the Lord thy God**, which brought thee forth out of the land of Egypt, from the house of bondage;
> 15 Who led thee through that great and terrible wilderness, wherein were fiery serpents, and scorpions, and drought, where there was no water; who brought thee forth water out of the rock of flint;
> 16 Who fed thee in the wilderness with manna,

which thy fathers knew not, that he might humble thee, and **that he might prove thee, to do thee good at thy latter end**;

17 And thou say in thine heart, My power and the might of mine hand hath gotten me this wealth.

18 But **thou shalt remember the Lord thy God**: for **it is he that giveth thee power to get wealth**, that he may establish his covenant which he sware unto thy fathers, as it is this day.

19 And it shall be, **if thou do at all forget the Lord thy God**, and walk after other gods, and serve them, and worship them, **I testify against you this day that ye shall surely perish**.

20 As the nations which the Lord destroyeth before your face, so shall ye perish; because ye would not be obedient unto the voice of the Lord your God. (Deuteronomy 8)

Unfortunately, the Israelites *did* forget God and how their wealth was obtained, which ruined it for everyone else in the future. In these last days, God is reluctant to grant fulfillment of the prophecies regarding that *Type*. He is concerned that granting those promises will corrupt the righteous when needed most. For this reason, we should be aware of and learn from the consequences of arrogance associated with this *Type* but *not* expect a financial windfall until The Millennium for those who will return and reign with Our Lord.

# POSTSCRIPT

There is a postscript to this: during the Last Revival, when God performs His *Final Work* bringing in His lost children, there will come such a hunger for things about God that those who fill the vacuum will likely experience significant financial profits. Let's pray they (and their support staff) don't succumb to the sin of ungrateful arrogance and lose their souls for the love of what money can buy.

# CONCLUSION

You can take the people out of Egypt, but you can't take Egypt out of everyone. That's one of the main messages from the account of Moses and the children of Israel. They were plagued by deceiving spirits from the religions surrounding them; they didn't live in a vacuum.

Despite the wonders God demonstrated on their behalf, most Israelites were guilty of murmuring continuously. According to the apostle Paul, everything that happened to the Israelites is a *Type* or an example that portends to things we will experience in our day, and he counseled us not to be ignorant of them but to learn from them and be ready for these things.

Here are the main *Types* addressed in this book:

- Bondage: don't crave carnal things, don't be Idolaters, don't worship false gods, avoid false religions, don't be fornicators, don't test God, don't murmur
- Their Feast Days
- Darkness (physical and spiritual)
- Parting of the Sea
- Split Rock of Horeb
- Fiery Serpents
- Eagles' Wings
- Lands of Promise
- Signs and Wonders

- Evidences of the Exodus
- The prophet like Moses
- The true nature of God
- The God of the Old Testament
- Deception

# HOW TO GET EGYPT OUT OF A PERSON?

How do you get Egypt out of a person? By the process of *repentance*. We were all born with God's Light, also called our *conscience*.

> 27 **The SPIRIT OF MAN is the CANDLE of the LORD, searching all the inward parts** of the belly. (Proverbs 20)

The individual conscience within each person is what guides them, whether they were taught God's laws or not.

> 15 Which **shew the work of the law written in their HEARTS, their CONSCIENCE also bearing witness**, and their thoughts the mean while accusing or else excusing one another; (Romans 2)

Most of us have been driven to repent or change due to unhappiness. That was my fate as well. When I turned to God at age 16, I had already been down the road of emotional and spiritual separation from God for 12 years.

19 **Who being PAST FEELING** have given themselves over unto lasciviousness, to work all uncleanness with greediness. (Ephesians 4)

I was coming out of my "Egypt" while others were entering theirs. It took three years to get the Egypt out of me entirely. The story of my coming to Christ is shared in my book TESTIMONY: *The Christian Writings & Testimonies of Arlin Ewald Nusbaum*. I was motivated to do missionary service to help others do the same. I had confidence that anyone could be restored to oneness with God.

Our Lord put it like this: *we must be born again.*

3 Jesus answered and said unto him, Verily, verily, I say unto thee, **Except a man be BORN AGAIN, he cannot see the kingdom of God**. (John 3)

Our Lord spent His ministry (and perhaps His entire pre-ministry life) teaching others how to be born again. This is why people study His teachings; they are full of tips, suggestions, stories, parables, etc., how to do that. He and His principles are described as the *Bread of Life*:

35 And Jesus said unto them, **I AM the BREAD of LIFE**: he that cometh to me **shall never hunger**; and he that believeth on me shall **never thirst**.
48 **I AM that BREAD of LIFE**.
51 **I AM the LIVING BREAD** which came down

from heaven: **if any man EAT of THIS BREAD, he shall LIVE FOR EVER**. (John 6)

The best way to remove Egypt from oneself is by keeping filled with the Bread of Life and putting on the Armour of God every day, as Paul taught.

> 11 **Put on the whole ARMOUR of GOD**, that ye may be able to stand against the wiles of the devil.
> 12 For we wrestle not against flesh and blood, but against principalities, against powers, against the rulers of the darkness of this world, against spiritual wickedness in high *places*.
> 13 Wherefore take unto you the **whole ARMOUR of GOD**, that ye may be able to withstand in the evil day, and having done all, to stand.
> 14 Stand therefore, having your **loins girt** about with **TRUTH,** and having on the **BREASTPLATE** of **RIGHTEOUSNESS;**
> 15 And your **feet shod** with the preparation of the **GOSPEL of PEACE;**
> 16 Above all, taking the **SHIELD** of **FAITH,** wherewith ye shall be able to quench all the fiery darts of the wicked.
> 17 And take the **HELMET** of **SALVATION,** and the **SWORD** of the **SPIRIT,** which is the **WORD of GOD**:
> 18 **Praying always** with all prayer and supplication in the Spirit, and **watching thereunto** with all perseverance and supplication for all saints; (Ephesians 6)

I pray you will take the name of Our Lord upon yourselves so that He can bless you, keep you, shine His face upon you, and be gracious to you. Let Him lift His countenance upon you and send you His peace. Amen.

# APPENDIX: SHEKINAH REFERENCES

## DEFINITIONS

**Easton's Bible Dictionary**

A Chaldee word meaning resting-place, not found in Scripture, but used by the later Jews to designate the visible symbol of God's presence in the tabernacle, and afterwards in Solomon's temple. When the Lord led Israel out of Egypt, he went before them "in a pillar of a cloud." This was the symbol of his presence with his people. For references made to it during the wilderness wanderings, see Exodus 14:20; 40:34-38; Leviticus 9:23, 24; Numbers 14:10; 16:19, 42. It is probable that after the entrance into Canaan this glory-cloud settled in the tabernacle upon the ark of the covenant in the most holy place. We have, however, no special reference to it till the consecration of the temple by Solomon, when it filled the whole house with its glory, so that the priests could not stand to minister (1 Kings 8:10-13; 2 Chronicles 5:13, 14; 7:1-3). Probably it remained in the first temple in the holy of holies as the symbol of Jehovah's presence so long as that temple stood. It afterwards disappeared.[1]

**Got Questions Ministries**

The word *shekinah* does not appear in the Bible, but the concept clearly does. The Jewish rabbis coined this extra-biblical expression, a form of a Hebrew word that literally means "he caused to dwell," signifying that it was a divine visitation of the presence or dwelling of the Lord God on this earth. The Shekinah was first evident when the Israelites set out from Succoth in their escape from Egypt. There the Lord appeared in a cloudy pillar in the day and a fiery pillar by night: "After leaving Succoth they camped at Etham on the edge of the desert. By day the LORD went ahead of them in a pillar of cloud to guide them on their way and by night in a pillar of fire to give them light, so that they could travel by day or night. Neither the pillar of cloud by day nor the pillar of fire by night left its place in front of the people" (Exodus 13:20-22).[2]

**International Standard Bible Encyclopedia**

she-ki'-na (shekhinah, "that which dwells," from the verb shakhen, or shakhan, "to dwell," "reside"): This word is not found in the Bible, but there are allusions to it in Isaiah 60:2 Matthew 17:5 Luke 2:9 Romans 9:4. It is first found in the Targums.[3]

**Webster's Revised Unabridged Dictionary**

(n.) The visible majesty of the Divine Presence, especially when resting or dwelling between the cherubim on the mercy seat, in the Tabernacle, or in the Temple of Solomon; — a term used in the Targums and by the later Jews, and adopted by Christians.[4]

## STRONG'S CONCORDANCE

## H3519

[Exo 29:43, Lev 9:23, 2Ch 7:1, Eze 9:3, Eze 10:18, Eze 11:22]

כָּבוֹד kâbôwd, kaw-bode'; rarely כָּבֹד kâbôd; from H3513; properly, weight, but only figuratively in a good sense, splendor or copiousness:—glorious(-ly), glory, honour(-able).

**c.** of God, *glory*, (1) in historic theophanies: to Moses Exodus 33:18, 22 (J); ‖ אֶת Numbers 14:22 (JE); ‖ ◇גָּדְלוֹ Deuteronomy 5:21. P uses יהוה כ׳ for theophanies of the Exodus Exodus 16:7, 10; Exodus 24:16, 17; Exodus 40:34, 35; Leviticus 9:6, 23; Numbers 14:10; Numbers 16:19; Numbers 17:7; Numbers 20:6, compare 2 Chronicles 5:14 = 1 Kings 8:11; 2 Chronicles 7:1, 2, 3; so Ezekiel, Ezekiel 1:28; Ezekiel 3:12, 23; Ezekiel 10:4 (twice in verse); Ezekiel 10:18; Ezekiel 11:23; Ezekiel 43:4, 5; Ezekiel 44:4; with the variation כ׳ אֱלֹהֵי יִשְׂרָאֵל Ezekiel 8:4; Ezekiel 9:3; Ezekiel 10:19; Ezekiel 11:22; Ezekiel 43:2, and הַכָּבוֹ◇ד Ezekiel 3:23; the sacred tent was sanctified by the Glory Exodus 29:43 (P), and the temple was כ׳ מִשְׁכַּן ◇מְקוֹם Psalm 26:8; when the ark was captured, the Glory went into exile from Israel 1 Samuel 4:21, 22. (2) *in historic and ideal* manifestations to the pious mind Yahweh's, name is a name of glory Psalm 72:19; Nehemiah 9:5; his eyes eyes of glory Isaiah 3:8; in the temple his glory is seen Psalm 63:3; it is על השמים Psalm 113:4; על כל הארץ Psalm 57:6; Psalm 57:12; in a thunderstorm he is אֵל הַכָּבוֹ◇ד Psalm 29:3; his glory is לְעוֹ◇לָם Psalm 104:31; it is great Psalm 138:5; above all the earth Psalm 108:6; the whole earth is full of it Isaiah 6:3 the heavens are declaring כְּבוֹ◇ד אֵל Psalm 19:2; with reference to the divine reign Psalm הֲדַר כ׳ הוֹ◇דֶךָ, Psalm 145:12; הֲדַר מַלְכוּתוֹ ◇ כ׳ 145:5. (3) he is מֶלֶךְ הַכָּבוֹ◇ד Psalm 24:7; Psalm 24:8; Psalm 24:9; Psalm 24:10 (twice in verse); he will appear in his glory Psalm 102:17, his glory will be revealed in a march through the wilderness to the holy land Isaiah 40:5, the land will see it Isaiah 35:2, shine with it Ezekiel 43:3, and it will dwell in the land Psalm 85:10; it will be to the rearward of Israel Isaiah 58:8; it will arise and be seen upon Jerusalem Isaiah 60:1, 2; Yahweh will be the glory in the midst of her Zechariah 2:9; the temple will be filled with it Haggai 2:7; the earth will be filled with a knowledge of it Habakkuk 2:14, and with it Numbers 14:21 (JE) Psalm 72:19; it will be declared among the nations and all will see it Isaiah 66:18, 19 (twice in verse); Psalm 97:6 and peoples and kings revere it Psalm 102:16; Isaiah 59:19; י׳ will reign before his elders in glory

Isaiah 24:23; the resting-place of the Messiah will be כָּבוֹד Isaiah 11:10.

# H6051

[Exo 40:34, Eze 10:3]

I. 87 עָנָן noun masculine Exodus 19:16 cloud-mass, cloud; (הֶעָ׳ absolute Exodus 19:9 +; construct עֲנַן Hosea 6:4 +; suffix עֲנָנְךָ Numbers 14:14, עֲנָנוֹ Job 26:9; Job 37:15; plural עָנִים Jeremiah 4:13;

**1.** *cloud-mass:*
**a.** especially of theophanic cloud (58 times), chiefly at Exodus in J E (less often P), usually עַמּוּד הֶעָ׳ Exodus 13:21, 22 + (see עַמּוּד), but also עָ׳ alone Exodus 34:5; compare Exodus 14:20 (J), Numbers 10:34; Numbers 11:35; Numbers 14:14 (all J E); עַב הֶעָ׳ Exodus 19:9, כְּבֵד עָ׳ Exodus 19:16 (E); עָ׳ in P Exodus 16:10; Exodus 24:15 23 times; also Deuteronomy 1:33; Deuteronomy 4:11; Deuteronomy 5:19; Psalm 78:14; Psalm 105:39; in temple 1 Kings 8:10, 11 2 Chronicles 5:13, 14, compare Ezekiel 1:4; Ezekiel 10:3, 4; hence in general Psalm 97:2, as symbol of protection Isaiah 4:5; as a barrier Lamentations 3:44; compare אֲבַק רַגְלָיו וְעָ׳ Nahum 1:3.

# G541

[Heb 1:3]

ἀπαύγασμα, -τος, τό, (from ἀπαυγάζω to emit

brightness, and this from αὐγή brightness; cf. ἀποσκίασμα, ἀπείκασμα, ἀπεικόνισμα, ἀπήχημα), reflected brightness: Christ is called in Hebrews 1:3 ἀπαύγ. τῆς δόξης τοῦ θεοῦ, inasmuch as he perfectly reflects the majesty of God; so that the same thing is declared here of Christ metaphysically, which he says of himself in an ethical sense in John 12:45 (John 14:9): ὁ θεωρῶν ἐμὲ θεωρεῖ τὸν πέμψαντά με. (Wis. 7:26; Philo, mund. opif. § 51; plant. Noë § 12; de concup. § 11; and often in ecclesiastical writings; see more fully in Grimm on Sap., the passage cited, p. 161f) [Some interpreters still adhere to the significant effulgence or radiance (as distinguished from refulgence or reflection), see Kurtz at the passage; Sophocles Lexicon, under the word; Cremer, under the word.]

# G1391

[Act 7:2, Rom 9:4, 2Pe 1:17]

δόξα dóxa, dox'-ah; from the base of G1380; glory (as very apparent), in a wide application (literal or figurative, objective or subjective):—dignity, glory(-ious), honour, praise, worship.

**1.** properly: τοῦ φωτός, Acts 22:11; of the sun, moon, stars, 1 Corinthians 15:40f; used of the heavenly brightness, by which God was conceived of as surrounded, Luke 2:9; Acts 7:55, and by which heavenly beings were surrounded when they appeared on earth, Luke

9:31; Revelation 18:1; with which the face of Moses was once made luminous, 2 Corinthians 3:7, and also Christ in his transfiguration, Luke 9:32; δόξα τοῦ κυρίου, in the Sept. equivalent to כְּבוֹד יְהוָה, in the Targum and Talmud שְׁכִינָה, Shekinah or Shechinah [see BB. DD. under the word], the glory of the Lord, and simply ἡ δόξα, a bright cloud by which God made manifest to men his presence and power on earth (Exodus 24:17; Exodus 40:28 (34ff), etc.): **Romans 9:4**; Revelation 15:8; Revelation 21:11, 23; hence, ὁ θεός τῆς δόξης (God to whom belongs δόξα) ὤφθη, **Acts 7:2**; Χερουβεὶν δόξης, on whom the divine glory rests (so δόξα, without the article, Exodus 40:28 (34); 1 Samuel 4:22; Sir. 49:8), Hebrews 9:5.

# G5316

[Rev 1:16]

φαίνω; (1 aorist active subjunctive 3 person singular φανῇ, L T WH in Revelation 8:12; Revelation 18:23 (see below and ἀναφαίνω; Winers Grammar, § 15, under the word; Buttmann, 41 (35))); passive, present φαίνομαι; 2 aorist ἐφαινην; 2 future φανήσομαι and (in 1 Peter 4:18) φανοῦμαι (cf. Kühner, § 343, under the word; (Veitch, under the word)); (φάω); in Greek writings from Homer down; to bring forth into the light, cause to shine; to show. In Biblical Greek:
1. Active intransitively, to shine, shed light

(which the Greeks (commonly (cf. Liddell and Scott, under the word, A. II.)) express by the passive), the Sept. for הֵאִיר: τό φῶς φαίνει, John 1:5; 1 John 2:8; ὁ λύχνος, John 5:35; 2 Peter 1:19 (1 Macc. 4:50; Genesis 1:17); ἥλιος, **Revelation 1:16**; ὁ ἥλιος καί ἡ σελήνη, Revelation 21:23; ἡ ἡμέρα, Revelation 8:12 Rec.

## AMPLIFIED BIBLE

43 There I will meet with the Israelites, and the Tent of Meeting shall be sanctified by **My glory** [the **Shekinah, God's dwelling presence**]. (Exodus 29:43 AMP)

34 Then the **cloud** [the **Shekinah, God's visible, dwelling presence**] **covered** the **Tent of Meeting**, and the **glory** and **brilliance** of the **LORD filled** the **tabernacle**. (Exodus 40:34 AMP)

23 Moses and Aaron went into the Tent of Meeting, and when they came out they blessed the people, and the **glory** and **brilliance** of the **LORD** [the **Shekinah cloud**] **appeared to all the people** [as promised]. (Leviticus 9:23 AMP)

1 When Solomon had finished praying, fire came down from heaven and consumed the burnt offering and the sacrifices, and the **[Shekinah] glory** and **brilliance** of the LORD **filled the house**. (2 Chronicles 7:1 AMP)

3 Then the **[Shekinah] glory** and **brilliance** of the God of Israel (the cloud) went up from the **cherubim on which it had rested**, to [stand above] the threshold of the [LORD'S] temple. And the LORD called to the man clothed with linen, who had the scribe's writing case at his side. (Ezekiel 9:3 AMP)

3 Now the cherubim were standing on the right side of the temple when the man entered; and **a cloud** [the **Shekinah glory of God**] **filled the inner courtyard.**
18 Then the **[Shekinah] glory** of the LORD departed from the threshold of the temple and rested over the cherubim. (Ezekiel 10:3, 18 AMP)

22 Then the cherubim lifted up their wings with the wheels beside them, and the **[Shekinah] glory** of the **God** of Israel **hovered over them.** (Ezekiel 11:22 AMP)

2 And he answered, "Brothers and fathers, listen to me! **The God of glory** [the **Shekinah, the radiance of God**] **appeared to our father Abraham** when he was in Mesopotamia, before he lived in Haran, (Acts 7:2 AMP)

4 who are Israelites, to whom belongs the adoption as sons, the **glory (Shekinah),** the [special] covenants [with Abraham, Moses, and David], the giving of the Law, the [system of temple] worship, and the [original] promises. (Romans 9:4 AMP)

3 The **Son is the radiance** and only expression of the **glory** of [our awesome] **God** [reflecting **God's Shekinah glory**, the **Light-being**, the **brilliant light of the divine**], and the exact representation and perfect imprint of **His [Father's] essence**, and upholding and maintaining and propelling all things [the entire physical and spiritual universe] by His powerful word [carrying the universe along to its predetermined goal]. When He [Himself and no other] had [by offering Himself on the cross as a sacrifice for sin] accomplished purification from sins and established our freedom from guilt, He sat down [revealing His completed work] at the right hand of the Majesty on high [revealing His Divine authority], (Hebrews 1:3 AMP)

17 For when He was invested with honor and [the **radiance of the Shekinah**] **glory** from **God the Father**, such a voice as this came to Him from the [splendid] **Majestic Glory** [in the **bright cloud** that **overshadowed Him,** saying], "This is My Son, My Beloved Son in whom I am well-pleased and delighted"– (2 Peter 1:17 AMP)

16 In His right hand He held seven stars, and from His mouth came a sharp two-edged sword [of judgment]; and **His face [reflecting His majesty** and the **Shekinah glory**] was **like the sun shining** in [all] its **power [at midday]**. (Revelation 1:16 AMP)

## NOTES

**Exo 29:43** This Hebrew word is not found in the Bible, but was used by the rabbis to describe the presence of God. Its basic meaning is "royal residence." Among other things, the rabbis said that the Shekinah is present where ten people pray together, or where three people are sitting as a court of judges.

**2Ch 7:1** This term is not found in the Bible, but was used by the ancient rabbis to refer to the divine presence.

**Eze 9:3** The word *Shekinah* does not appear in the Bible, but it was used by ancient Jews to refer to the physical presence of God among men; usually the *Shekinah glory*.

**Rom 9:4** The Hebrew word "Shekinah" ("divine presence") does not appear in Scripture, but has been used by both Christians and Jews to describe the visible Presence of God (the brilliant light of the divine), in such things as the burning bush, the cloud and the pillar of fire that led the Hebrews in the wilderness, and the Presence of God that rested between the cherubim over the mercy seat of the ark. It is said in the Talmud that the Emperor Hadrian once told a rabbi, "I want to see your God." The rabbi replied, "You cannot see him." "Indeed," said the Emperor, "I will see him." So the rabbi took the Emperor and positioned him to face the sun during the summer solstice, and said to him, "Look at it." He replied, "I am not able to." The rabbi said, "If you are not able to look at the sun, which is merely one of the servants that attend the Holy One–blessed be He–then how can you presume to look at the divine presence!"

**Heb 1:3** The word "Shekinah" does not appear in Scripture, but has been used by both Christians and Jews to describe the visible divine Presence of God, in such things as the burning bush, the cloud and the pillar of fire that led the Hebrews in the wilderness, and the Presence of God that rested between the cherubim over the mercy seat of the ark.

**2Pe 1:17** The word "Shekinah" does not appear in Scripture, but has been used by both Christians and Jews to describe the visible divine Presence of God (the brilliant light of the divine), in such things as the burning bush, the cloud and the pillar of fire that led the Hebrews in the wilderness, and the Presence of God that rested between the cherubim over the mercy seat of the ark.

**Rev 1:16** The visible, divine Presence.[5]

# WIKIPEDIA

Shekhinah (Hebrew: שְׁכִינָה, Modern: Šəḵīna, Tiberian: Šeḵīnā) is the English transliteration of a Hebrew word meaning "dwelling" or "settling" and denotes the presence of God in a place. This concept is found in Judaism and the Torah, as mentioned in Exodus 25:8. The word "Shekhinah" is not found in the Bible. It appears in the Mishnah, the Talmud, and Midrash.

## Etymology

The word *shekhinah* is first encountered in the rabbinic literature. The Semitic root from which *shekhinah* is derived, š-k-n, means "to settle, inhabit, or dwell". In the verb form, it is often used to refer to the dwelling of a person or animal in a place, or to the dwelling of God. Nouns derived from the root included *shachen* ("neighbor") and *mishkan* (a dwelling-place, whether a secular home or a holy site such as the Tabernacle).

## In Judaism

While shekhinah is a feminine word in Hebrew, it primarily seemed to be featured in masculine or androgynous contexts referring to a divine manifestation of the presence of God, based especially on readings of the Talmud.

## Manifestation

The prophets made numerous references to visions of the presence of God, particularly in the context of the Tabernacle or Temple, with figures such as thrones or robes filling the Sanctuary. The *shekhinah* is referred to as manifest in the Tabernacle and the Temple in Jerusalem throughout rabbinic literature. It is also reported as being present in other contexts:

- While a person (or people) study Torah, the Shekhinah is among them.
- "Whenever ten are gathered for prayer, there the Shekhinah rests."
- "When three sit as judges, the Shekhinah is with them."
- Cases of personal need: "The Shekhinah dwells over the headside of the sick man's bed", "Wheresoever they were exiled, the Shekhinah went with them."
- "A man and woman – if they merit, the Shekhinah is between them. If not, fire consumes them." According to one interpretation of this source, the Shekhinah is the highest of six types of holy fire. When a married couple is worthy of this manifestation, all other types of fire are consumed by it.:111, n. 4
  The Talmud states that "the Shekhinah rests on man neither through gloom, nor through sloth, nor through frivolity, nor through levity, nor through talk, nor through idle chatter, but only through a matter of joy in connection with a mitzvah."

There is no occurrence of the word "shekhinah" in pre-rabbinic literature such as the Dead Sea Scrolls. It is only afterwards in the targums and rabbinic literature that the Hebrew term *shekhinah*, or Aramaic equivalent *shekinta*, is found, and then becomes extremely common. Martin McNamara (see notes) considers that the absence might lead to the conclusion that the term only originated after the destruction of the temple in 70 CE, but notes 2 Maccabees 14:35 "a temple for your habitation", where the Greek text (Koinē Greek: ναὸν τῆς σῆς σκηνώσεως) suggests a possible parallel understanding, and where σκήνωσις *skēnōsis* "a tent-building", a variation on an early loanword from Phoenician (Ancient Greek: ἡ σκηνή *skēnē* "tent"), is deliberately used to represent the original Hebrew or Aramaic term.

## Jewish prayers

The 17th blessing of the daily *Amidah* prayer concludes with the line "[Blessed are You, God,] who returns His Presence (*shekhinato*) to Zion" (הַמַּחֲזִיר שְׁכִינָתוֹ לְצִיּוֹן). The Liberal Jewish prayer-book for Rosh Hashanah and Yom Kippur (*Machzor Ruach Chadashah*) contains a creative prayer based on Avinu Malkeinu, in which the feminine noun shekhinah is used in the interests of gender neutrality.[6]

# Notes

1. https://biblehub.com/topical/s/shechinah.htm.
2. https://www.gotquestions.org/shekinah-glory.html.
3. https://biblehub.com/topical/s/shekinah.htm.
4. Ibid.
5. https://www.blueletterbible.org/search/search.cfm?Criteria=shekinah&t=AMP.
6. https://en.wikipedia.org/wiki/Shekhinah.

www.ingramcontent.com/pod-product-compliance
Lightning Source LLC
Chambersburg PA
CBHW070240090526
44586CB00035B/1084